Praise for *Greekonomics*

"The future of the euro matters hugely to everyone in Europe, whether we are in or out of the single currency. I worked closely with Vicky Pryce when I was in government, and I am delighted that she has produced this book on the economic and political issue of the moment."
Peter Mandelson

"The deeper causes of Greece's prolonged crisis have been poorly understood by European policymakers and global commentators alike. Many tended to look at the symptoms, the debt and deficit, rather than the structural problems and in particular the need for reorganisation and transparent management of the Greek state. Furthermore wider systemic problems of the eurozone that affected Greece (and not only) were overlooked or underestimated. This resulted in austerity being prioritised over reform. My view has always been that this was to be an inappropriate prescription; one that was also politically very difficult as it carried a sense of injustice. This book offers a fresh perspective on the underlying causes of Greece's economic crisis, and the challenges looming ahead, as seen from the eyes of a Greek-born international economist."
Former Greek Prime Minister, George Papandreou

REFERENCE

"Vicky Pryce, like me, had the sometimes unenviable job when she worked in government as Joint Head of the Government Economic Service of advising ministers on the economic implications of different policy options. While I was Head of the Treasury she contributed to the UK's five economic tests for joining the euro, working with my team. In this important book, she turns her attention to the current crisis in Europe and particularly how it has affected her country of birth, and in the process reminds us that political decisions without strong economic foundations can all too easily turn sour."
Gus O'Donnell

"The UK's relationship with a currency union within Europe has always been problematic, as I learned from my experience. I therefore very much welcome Vicky Pryce's book which is exploring further the political and economic thinking in Europe and the serious problems that the single currency has created across the continent."
Norman Lamont

"Vicky Pryce worked with me first at the DTI and then as part of the Officials Group of the National Economic Council which we set up to advise on the UK's response to the biggest economic and financial crisis since the 1930s. I am delighted she has used that experience to give her own personal perspective on the eurozone crisis."
Alistair Darling

GREEKONOMICS

GREEKONOMICS
THE EURO CRISIS AND WHY POLITICIANS DON'T GET IT
VICKY PRYCE

Biteback Publishing

This edition published in Great Britain in 2013 by
Biteback Publishing Ltd
Westminster Tower
3 Albert Embankment
London SE1 7SP
Copyright © Vicky Pryce 2013

isbn 978-1-84954-628-7

10 9 8 7 6 5 4 3 2 1

A CIP catalogue record for this book is available from the British Library.

Set in Sabon

Printed and bound in Great Britain by
CPI Group (UK) Ltd, Croydon CR0 4YY

MIX
Paper from
responsible sources
FSC® C020471

CONTENTS

PREFACE

I was compelled to write this book and offer my take on the eurozone crisis after finding myself the only economist in London who had anything positive to say about the Greeks. It became clear that the financial crisis of the late 2000s, which Alistair Darling was among the first to refer to as 'the worst economic crisis since the 1930s', was far from conquered and its reverberations were in fact continuing to engulf most of Europe. Dealing with the crisis required substantial state intervention, particularly to save the banking system, economies went into decline and countries like Greece started sinking under the weight of hugely rising debt and uncontrollable deficits. There seemed to be little sympathy for the hardship of the ordinary Greek citizen as Greece drifted into the worst recession ever seen under strict austerity measures imposed on it by the 'troika' of the International Monetary Fund, the European Commission and the European Central Bank. There were serious discussions about whether the Greeks should ever have been allowed to join the euro in 2001, let alone the European Union, and there have been numerous programmes focusing on the Greek economy and its inability to manage itself. I participated in one such programme shown on Channel 4, entitled *Be Greek for a Week*, which invited people in the UK to experience the abuses of the Greek system. The stereotype, or shall I call it a caricature, of the Greeks began to emerge: Greeks formed a lazy, pampered and corrupt nation where bribery was rife; its citizens were unwilling to pay taxes and received large welfare benefits, were encouraged to take well-paid early retirement and thus enjoyed long siestas and periods in the sun. I did wonder at times, when reading the UK and German press in particular, whether this was just jealousy because of the nicer weather in Greece. But it was still astonishing to read reports of Germans cancelling their holidays to Greece in protest at the Greeks' supposed profligacy. As if that would help! I felt that some more explanation was needed, not just about the economics of the single currency and its impact on countries like Greece, but also about the cultural and historical background to the country, which might shed some light upon where the Greeks are coming from in all this.

Climate, of course, matters. It shapes mood, working hours and the activities we participate in. Nine years ago, my daughter was a torch bearer at the 2004 Games in Athens. Then, the weather was glorious and watching the beach volleyball final by the seaside under a full moon was amazing. Bits of the road infrastructure were completed just a few days before the Games started – not because of cracks on the motorway (as discovered just a few days before the start of the 2012 London Olympic Games) but because as construction teams dug they seemed to hit on ancient burial grounds and other archaeological artefacts. This stopped work for long periods at a time while the artefacts were inspected, collected and shipped into museums. But everything went smoothly in the end and visitors found the going easy, the people very friendly and the festival atmosphere infectious. It was also the summer when Greece won the Euro 2004 football tournament, completely against the odds. A year later, Greece also won the European basketball championship and, amazingly, the Eurovision Song Contest! The Greeks, like the Brits at the end of the 2012 Games, felt on top of the world.

But the 2004 Olympics brought the beginning of the downward cycle in Greek finances. There was a huge amount of expenditure to upgrade the transport infrastructure and security costs had rocketed. Greece continued to overspend after the Olympics, encouraged by the availability of cheap money. The politicians wasted the Games legacy and corruption and inefficiency were allowed to fester while the rest of Europe looked away. When the crisis hit, there was little to fall back on.

So from heroes to villains! The Greeks are now cast as the main threat to the euro's survival. But remember that the ordinary citizen has seen a massive decline in living standards, that bankruptcies and suicides are rising alarmingly, and that Greece now has one of the highest unemployment and poverty rates in Europe. People are desperate. They need hope and they need jobs, and they need tourists! So if you are visiting the country think of Greece as the cradle of democracy; marvel at the sites where art, theatre, poetry, philosophy and science flourished; soak in the sun and enjoy the hospitality of people who, despite seeing their incomes fall for a fifth year running, remain on balance among the most welcoming and generous in the world.

It is true that the Greek system is screaming for reform. But the analysis so far has been too simplistic and the solution – austerity – too narrow-minded. What has become obvious is that this is not a Greek crisis but a crisis of the euro project as a whole. Since the Lehman collapse, sovereign bond yields have rocketed for many countries in the eurozone to unsustainable levels. Portugal, Ireland and Greece, and now also Spain and Cyprus, have sought bail-outs of some sort or another. Austerity programmes of dubious effectiveness have been instigated across Europe, leading to stagnation in the continent overall and declines in many other countries. Nobel Prize economists such as Joseph Stiglitz and Paul Krugman have questioned the wisdom of abandoning Keynesian economics for austerity, causing an orchestrated coordinated decline in activity when the state cuts back at the same time as companies and individuals who have borrowed a lot retrench. But there were no mechanisms to hand when the crisis struck because the euro was allowed to be created without the leaders of the European Union realising its fundamental flaws. The result is that ordinary people in many of these countries are now suffering the worst cuts in their living standards since the Second World War, with serious social and political consequences.

Putting this book together was only possible through a series of interviews, here in the UK and abroad. In the UK, I am particularly grateful to Norman Lamont, Peter Mandelson, Alistair Darling, former Cabinet Secretary Gus O'Donnell, Charles Grant, Tim Garton-Ash, Sony Kapoor and Meghnad Desai. I have also scoured the publications of numerous think tanks such as Chatham House, Mark Leonard's European Council for Foreign Relations (ECFR), Andrew Hilton's Centre for Financial Services Innovation (CFSI), Charles Grant's Centre for European Reform (CER), and David Marsh's Official Monetary and Financial Institutions Forum (OMFIF). Examples of European think tanks include Bruegel in Brussels, Real Instituto Elcano in Madrid and the IFO institute in Munich, whose President, Professor Sinn, has also kindly offered comments. Great books such as David Marsh's *The Euro* have been of help as well as Kiron Sarkar's excellent blog and the Hellenic Observatory publications at the London School of Economics (LSE) run by Kevin Featherstone. In addition, LSE academic Dr Waltraud Schelkle has provided views from a German perspective. In Greece, I have spoken to numerous current and past policy makers and politicians, including ex-Finance Minister George Alogoskoufis, ex-Deputy Finance and Deputy Foreign Minister Petros Doukas, ex-Cabinet Minister Louka Katseli and former Greek Prime Minister George Papandreou. I also want to thank the various businesses around Europe that have given me their views on the crisis as well as the Organisation for Economic Co-operation and Development (OECD) and the European Commission, particularly the EU Task Force for Greece, for having been so helpful with their information and data.

For much of the era that saw the euro move from drawing board to working currency, I was employed as a government economist and finally as Joint Head of the UK Government Economic Service with Dave Ramsden at the Treasury. I spent many hours discussing the euro question with dedicated professional economists working in both the public and private sector. This book has been informed by those discussions.

Finally I want to thank the team that helped me make this book possible, in particular Mark Beatson, Ed Beesley, Ava Alleyne, Boni Sones, George Courmouzis, Lydia Argyropoulos and the brilliant Biteback Publishing team who nagged me every day and kept me going. Many thanks also to Chris Osborne for his encouragement and support, and to my family, who put up with me while I was writing this book.

1

INTRODUCTION

In 1967, a shadowy group of officers known as 'the Colonels' staged a military coup and began their seven-year rule over Greece. I was still at school then but instantly decided that I would leave Greece as soon as possible and, a few years later, I moved from Athens to London. I wasn't one of the many young Greeks from a relatively privileged background who wanted to study abroad, intending to return to Greece afterwards. Instead I left determined to use the education I would acquire as a passport to try my luck elsewhere in Europe. The economy in Greece was in a dire state with sectors like tourism, within which my father worked, devastated by foreigners boycotting Greece in protest against the regime. And frankly, for much of my early years in the UK, I felt a sense of shock at seeing men in uniform rule a country still referred to as the cradle of democracy.

And yet I owe my love of economics to those terrible years of dictatorship. It was assumed that after my secondary education at the German School of Athens, which had been closed after the war and then reopened in 1952, I would attend university in Germany as lots of Greeks did in those days. As a teenager, however, I had been sent by my father to a summer school in Reading to improve my English, which was fast becoming the dominant foreign language. Instead of studying at the school, I followed a bunch of French girls on their daily trips to London and spent most of the time walking up and down the King's Road marvelling at the culture and the outfits (it was the period of hot pants!). The rest, as they say, is history. It had to be London and nowhere else and the London School of Economics was the only place to study. My always obliging father hired a well-known economics professor, Sakis Karagiorgas, who had to stop teaching at the University of Athens because of his left-wing views during the Colonels' regime but came highly recommended (a surprise to me, as my father was rather right-wing in those days). I started having lessons with him in the evenings after attending my German day school. The summer after my course had finished, I distinctly remember hearing on the radio that this same professor had been arrested following a bomb explosion in the basement of his house, where all my lessons had been held, and that in the process he had lost part of his hand! It seems that, all the time I was learning about economics, I was sitting above a bomb factory! He and his co-conspirators, including Vassilis Rapanos (who later held the post of President of the Board of the National

Bank of Greece and, very briefly, the post of Finance Minister after the 17 June 2012 elections before resigning due to ill health), seemed to have all been jailed together. Vassilis Rapanos later said in a newspaper interview that he had learned his economics in jail while in adjoining cells with the very same professor.

Sakis Karagiorgas and Vassilis Rapanos were both later released. In 1974, the Colonels got Greece involved in a disastrous attempt to annex Cyprus, which resulted in a Turkish invasion of the island and its resultant partition. The regime in Greece promptly fell and its leaders were tried and imprisoned. Professor Karagiorgas resumed his academic life and became a well-known economics professor. A period of renewal started with the release from prison (and return from exile) of former politicians, leading to Greece's eventual membership of the European Economic Community (EEC) in 1981 and then entry into the euro in 2001. Both were politically motivated and the Greeks were especially keen to join the EEC given their precarious geographical position. On the border, the Communist Balkans reminded the Greeks of the civil war of 1946–9, which saw Greece almost become part of the Soviet bloc. Across the sea was arch-enemy Turkey, which under the Ottoman empire had ruled Greece for 400 years until the early 1800s. Memories of the forced evacuation of millions of Greeks from Asia Minor after the First World War still rankle. Greece was also not too far across the water from a tumultuous Middle East and, to the south, northern Africa, rarely a haven of stability. Being embraced by Europe was a sign that Greece had been accepted into the club of developed, democratic countries and would ensure its undemocratic past was firmly behind it.

All of Greece cheered. As a Greek abroad who had been ashamed of what had been going on under the Colonels, I could hold my head up high again. There were concerns, however, that, in the rush to accept Greece into the EEC, there was insufficiently rigorous scrutiny of its political system, its still developing market economy and the ability of its rather inefficient institutions, particularly the public sector and the banks, to nurture and support a move to an open competitive economy. Other countries thought Greece was too small to be a real threat to their economic interests, with countries like France more worried about the threat posed by greater competition in agriculture from later EEC members such as Spain.

Still, European Community – and, from 1993, European Union (EU) – membership brought benefits: barriers to trade were progressively removed and the movement of people and capital flows expanded. The Greeks enjoyed a period of rapid growth. I saw my family regain their earlier affluent status and flourish. Various sectors of the economy did very well, particularly shipping and tourism, and prosperity grew unhindered. This rapid development, however, obscured the structural flaws that still existed in Greece.

THE EURO WAS A POLITICAL PROJECT

Joining the euro in 2001 made a lot less sense than joining the European Community, as Greece only met some of the criteria set for demonstrating convergence and suitability for the euro – and only with some fiddling of the figures. But Greece's eurozone partners were complicit in its entry – they wanted Greece in.

The need to unify Europe after the Second World War and ensure that conflict would never happen again gave rise to the Coal and Steel Community in the 1950s and progressed further with increasing efforts to achieve a single market in Europe throughout the 1980s. The benefits of the single market were well documented in the Cecchini Report[†] (to which I also contributed in my early days at the accounting and consulting firm KPMG, which I joined as Chief Economist in 1986, later becoming a partner). A single market for goods across the EU became a reality in the early 1990s, though services lagged behind. In bringing down tariffs, reducing price levels, achieving greater harmonisation of product regulation, allowing markets to function and enabling free movement of people, the single market was a great achievement. It was clear that the whole of Europe would benefit from lower inflation, higher investment, easier capital movements and the creation of a powerful trading bloc to rival the US and the growing challenge from China.

---

† Chaired by Paolo Cecchini, this 1988 report examined the benefits and costs of creating a single market in Europe, in accordance with provisions of the Treaty of Rome.

But the end of the Berlin Wall in 1989 and German reunification came at a huge price. The cost to Germany itself was enormous. It has been claimed that as much as €1.3trn was transferred from the West to rebuild the East, with money transfers still occurring. Reunification led to many years of poor growth as the East German economy was shaken up and forced to adapt slowly to the market economy of West Germany – and the rest of Europe. Although the population in general was behind reunification it had the side effect of exhausting the German taxpayers' patience with bailing out unproductive countries – which East Germany at that time was perceived to be. It also bound Germany into embarking on a euro project that put it firmly at the heart of Europe.

Creating a monetary union was principally a political project, not an economic one. It is a myth to think that there can be a pure economic union. All economies require rules to operate and these rules are set by politicians – democratic or authoritarian. Intent on ensuring that Germany did not use its might as Europe's biggest country to outdo the rest, the euro project was pushed aggressively to bind Germany to its neighbours and reduce the power of the Bundesbank (the German central bank). The political objective was to tie Germany's competitiveness and prospects to those of the rest of Europe and not allow it to expand at other countries' expense. But monetary union was also seen as the way to achieve eventual political union by the back door. Arguably political union should have come first and economic union would follow. However, it was too early at that stage to go down that route as countries were not then ready for deeper political integration. The process did result nevertheless in countries losing some of their sovereignty, including Germany, something which was probably not entirely appreciated in advance by the electorate. There was, in fact, relatively little public debate about joining the euro at the time. Right until the euro came into being, the majority of Germans wanted the Deutschmark to remain. But the German political élites – of right and left – were worried that if a new mighty Germany emerged, old fears would resurface. The truth is that from 1950 onwards Germany had agreed to share or pool part of its sovereignty with its neighbours. The euro was seen by policy makers as just another step in that process of European integration.

Nevertheless, in order to justify the move to a single currency as an economic project and as the next natural step towards full economic integration, various studies were commissioned by the European Commission and books were written at the time outlining some of the benefits of an economic and monetary union. They argued that removing exchange rate costs and currency uncertainties would reduce the transaction costs involved in trade across borders and encourage greater movement of goods, services, capital and people. Charles Grant, of the Centre for European Reform in London, thinks that despite the fact that politics kept the euro momentum going, the economics were already well understood to tilt the balance of thinking in favour of the euro. Keeping the Exchange Rate Mechanism (ERM) – a system introduced in March 1979, linking European currencies together within agreed bands – as a permanent alternative would have meant, in the longer run, restricting capital movements to prevent constant pressure on those currencies within the ERM.

The euro would thus become a new international reserve currency with the benefits that this brought in its wake. But, except within a limited circle of politicians and senior officials, there was very little questioning or debate about this in Europe. Many of these benefits make sense and are valid if the countries that come together are able to converge (and there is a proper unified system of regulation in the financial sector to avoid bubbles emerging). In reality, despite some obvious merits, this was a political project sold as an economic one to the electorates across Europe. In the rush to bind Germany into a union covering most of the countries in Europe, very little thought was given to whether the result might bear any resemblance to an optimal currency area. Countries were admitted without consulting their electorates but also without seriously questioning their ability to adapt to a very different environment where the fiscal and monetary policy options available to them became severely limited.

So we ended up with a monetary union as a preamble to a political union that consisted of countries that simply did not form an optimal currency area. Greece was one of these countries. Interest rates were set by the European Central Bank (ECB) for the eurozone as a whole and the result in many countries was lower real interest rates, both for the government and also for companies and individuals – and the Greeks, like other countries, went on a spending spree. After all, they were now part of a large domestic market with a single currency; they no longer needed to worry about the balance of payments and falls in the value of their currency which had restrained them in the past. Something that is often forgotten in the current debate is that German exports to the 'periphery' countries of the eurozone (mainly in the south) rose substantially after the euro was created. And as wages started to rise in the poorer countries, something that was always meant to happen as a way of achieving economic convergence, unit labour costs rose across most of southern Europe, while those of Germany were stagnant or even declining as Germany itself implemented long overdue labour market reforms. German labour competitiveness in relation to its eurozone partners improved. The competitiveness of German exports to the rest of the world also improved thanks to the external value of the euro being kept down by the inclusion of many less competitive periphery economies in the eurozone.

MEMBERSHIP OF THE EURO LED TO GREECE'S ECONOMIC CRISIS

But Greece had not invested in increasing the productive capacity of its economy and rapidly lost competitiveness. Who, therefore, is to blame? Interestingly, when the Greek nation expressed a real desire to join the EEC and then the euro, they were in reality secretly hoping that the Brussels bureaucrats would take over and free them from the control of their politicians, who they regarded as corrupt. Educated Greeks longed for a 'technocratic' government that would move them away from a rather Soviet-style economy subject to numerous controls and closed shops that killed entre-preneurship and discouraged initiative. Instead, very little attention was paid to what Greece was doing or to the worsening imbalances in trade, for example. As low interest rates and increasing wages fuelled strong consumer-led growth, the public sector grew to vast proportions. The number of state employees ballooned to 712,000 in a country with only eleven million people, many of these state employees recruited as political favours by the two main parties, the socialist Pasok and the right-wing New Democracy, that had run Greece since the departure of the Colonels. Corruption became endemic, tax avoidance and evasion the norm, and public spending grew out of control, with ineffi-ciency widespread. When the global financial crisis hit in 2008, Greece had nothing to fall back on and the adjustment has been extremely painful. The conditions attached to the two bail-outs for Greece of €110bn in May 2010 and €130bn in February 2012 have led to living standards being slashed. Public sector wages and pensions have been cut by some 25–30% on average since the start of the crisis, with far deeper reductions for some categories of pensioners.

Lucas Papademos, formerly Governor at the Bank of Greece and then Vice-President of the ECB, and who was briefly Greece's technocratic Prime Minister from November 2011 to May 2012, negotiated the second bail-out before the 6 May elections. In an interview in March 2012, he argued that the measures undertaken so far, which had been quite drastic, had already improved competitiveness and restored around half of what had been lost vis-à-vis Greece's eurozone partners in the previous nine years. This was before the latest set of labour market reforms had started to be implemented. This is good news for competitiveness but it is appalling to think of how all the gains in living standards made during the euro era have just been wiped out. It seems that hope has all but gone. By May 2013 unemployment stood at 27.6% of the working population and youth unemployment at 64.9%, both rates the highest in Europe. Although figures for Spain closely follow, the rates compare with a euro-area average of 12.1% and 23.3% respectively. It is reported that, since 2009, some 25% of all Greek companies have gone bust and that a similar percentage of small firms find it difficult to meet payments. Suicide rates have rocketed as poverty becomes widespread. Before 2009, Greece had one of the lowest suicide rates in the world – 2.8 per 100,000 people. A 40% rise in the first half of 2010 was reported by the health ministry and experts now say that the Greek suicide rate has probably doubled to about 5 per 100,000 people. For the first time Greeks, and not just illegal immigrants, are joining the queues for the soup kitchens. The latest notification I saw of where free food is being distributed in greater Athens listed 103 locations and another thirteen in Piraeus. When I was visiting my sister's home on election day on 6 May 2012, she and her friends were busy arranging food leftovers in Tupperware boxes to take to various families so they could feed their children. A year later, although many of the foreigners they were feeding had gone, either voluntarily or following arrest and deportation, the numbers of Greeks asking for help had swollen. Increasingly, the Greeks find themselves jobless and homeless, with a welfare system unable to support them.

WILL GREECE EXIT THE EURO?

The human cost of the last few years in Greece has been enormous. Data for the first quarter of 2013 show that the total output (GDP) was down on a year earlier by 5.3% and in the second quarter 3.8%, less than had been forecast as tourism receipts soared. But this will be the sixth successive year of decline as output fell by 6.4% in 2012, 6.9% in 2011, 3.5% in 2010, 3.2% in 2009 and 0.2% in 2008. Wages in the public sector have now fallen by more than 35% since the beginning of the crisis, pensions have been cut drastically and the minimum wage has been slashed by 22% for most workers and by 32% for those under twenty-five.

In 2012, increasing social tensions and violent demonstrations were extensively covered by the world media, who watched with amazement as a western country imploded. It was therefore hardly surprising that the only clear vote in the inconclusive general elections of 6 May 2012 was against austerity and the political parties responsible for it being inflicted on the Greek people. The voters brought an end to the two-party system of New Democracy and Pasok but gave no party an absolute majority. The great surprise was that the anti-austerity Syriza party (the Coalition of the Radical Left) came second, after New Democracy, with Pasok trailing a poor third. Many votes went to a host of smaller parties that either failed to make the 3% threshold required to be represented in Parliament or were represented in insufficient numbers individually to make a difference to the overall political arithmetic – including, in the latter category, the election to Parliament of members of the neo-Fascist Golden Dawn party. No coalition could therefore be formed and new elections were announced. The world shivered as the implications of a possible Greek exit – or 'Grexit' as it has now become known – began to sink in. The whole of the eurozone was affected. Spanish and Italian bond yields started to rise again and the break-up of the whole euro project started to seem possible, with the markets failing to be convinced that the political leadership of the eurozone could develop and implement a credible solution to the crisis despite numerous summits.

The fresh Greek elections held on 17 June 2012 were billed by the media as holding the key to the euro's continued existence. All eyes turned to Greece and in the process the various Greek leaders became household names across Europe: Antonis Samaras, of the New Democracy party; Evangelos Venizelos, from Pasok; and Alexis Tsipras, the charismatic young leader of Syriza.

As the election campaign got under way political leaders, all speaking rather good English, were interviewed in the wonderful sunshine beloved by the tourists and the discussions seemed to be conducted relatively calmly and with composure. Christine Lagarde, Managing Director of the IMF, irritated the Greeks by chastising them for not paying their taxes and hinted that she worried a lot less about the hardship of the Greeks by comparison to starving children in Africa. When it was revealed that she did not pay any tax herself as she is employed by the IMF, an international organisation that does not fall under any jurisdiction for tax purposes, the Greeks reacted angrily and Greek newspapers went to town in their attacks on Lagarde's comments. To add insult to injury, the British Prime Minister, David Cameron, was heard discussing contingency border control plans should Greece exit the euro, fearing that millions of Greeks would abandon their homeland and travel to the UK for work, causing even more chaos at passport control desks. Christine Lagarde or David Cameron may have thought they were stating the obvious but, for Greeks living on the edge of nervous exhaustion, every chance remark from abroad assumed gigantic proportions.

But in a way such criticism and speculation might have been helpful, as it concentrated the minds of the voters in the edgy period before they went back to the polls. The May 2012 election had produced a giant protest vote. The result of the 17 June rerun showed that protest and rejection of austerity remained powerful voices, but they were accompanied by a realisation that Greece needed a working government. It was clear the Greeks did not want to leave the euro and the world's reaction over the previous six weeks had scared them. They also felt they had been mocked for their democratic choices. At the election, Syriza's share of the vote increased again and it came a close second, but New Democracy (under Antonis Samaras) was the largest party and was able to form a coalition with the third-ranking Pasok and a small left-of-centre party, the Democratic Left (DIMAR). The coalition announced its intention to work to honour the spirit of the bail-out but hoped to renegotiate some of its conditions, especially the speed of fiscal consolidation (spending cuts, tax increases and privatisation revenues) given the dramatic decline of the economy.

People's faith in the system has taken a dive. Whenever possible Greeks either continue to move money abroad or keep their euros under their mattresses. Armed burglaries, until now unknown in Greece, are becoming commonplace as a result. People are not spending or investing and the economy appears in free-fall.

It is true that the Greeks, in dealing with their European partners, have generally not helped themselves. This has put the Greeks into the category of being ungovernable and untrustworthy negotiating partners. The Greeks' inability to implement what they had promised to do under the terms of the first bail-out package of May 2010 did not endear them to the Brussels bureaucrats or the IMF when they were negotiating the second bail-out. The Organisation for Economic Co-operation and Development report on the Greek administrative system of spring 2012 is one of the most damning indictments of any developed country that I have seen in more than three decades of professional experience as an economist, including working in Third-World countries and European states poorer than Greece. There has been some recent progress, particularly in the area of tax collection, but few public servants have been fired. While in Greece in August 2013, I experienced the OECD's indictment of the inefficiencies of Greek bureaucracy first-hand. I successfully managed to apply for a foreign resident's tax number online and assumed that this meant some bureaucracy had finally been cut. I was horrified to discover that I still had to appear in person to collect my number from a tiny airless office in central Athens, along with hundreds of others, some of whom had queued from 6 a.m. ahead of the office opening at 8 a.m.

The Samaras government nevertheless can claim with justification that it was voted in democratically with a mandate to renegotiate a crippling debt. Samaras knew that continued talk about a euro exit would be destabilising. A few weeks after the June elections, for example, David Cameron was reported to have reiterated that it could be in the UK's interests to block Greek citizens from entering the UK if Greece were to be forced out of the single currency – although such a move would appear to be illegal under European law provided that Greece remained within the EU! What Samaras and his new widely respected Finance Minister Yannis Stournaras achieved was to convince the other EU leaders that they were serious about reform. As a result, prospects of an imminent Greek exit faded from the headlines and the country was visited in 2013 by the German Chancellor Angela Merkel and her Finance Minister Wolfgang Schäuble in a demonstration of solidarity. But the fundamental problems that Greece's membership of the euro has brought have not gone away.

How easy it is to forget that the single market was the original cornerstone of the EEC and one that has taken decades to get as near to it as we are now, a single market which includes the freedom of movement of people across countries. A number of EU members such as Poland have been enjoying the ability to work across Europe without for the moment being part of the eurozone. David Cameron has forgotten a few facts. For one, the unemployment rate in Greece is not very different, including youth unemployment, to that in Spain, a much larger country with a vastly larger working population than tiny Greece. Why not talk about this instead? And what's more, he needn't worry too much as the Brits tend to underestimate the young Greeks' attachments to their mother's cooking as well as to seeing the sun occasionally.

As *The Economist* noted laconically in late July 2012, when the heat turned on Spain, 'moderating austerity programmes is a priority'. There followed more articles expressing concern about what was being imposed on European countries in the name of fiscal consolidation, including by the celebrated Nobel prize-winner Paul Krugman, who took up the anti-austerity baton. The IMF itself admitted in July 2013 that it may have underestimated the impact of the fiscal tightening on the economies in Europe, particularly in Greece, and in mid-2013 it criticised the European Commission's competence in handling the Greek crisis. Alas, this wisdom was not at the time uppermost in the minds of those who required Greece to accept a reduction in income and social justice as great as any imposed in post-war Europe. Combined with this imposed poverty we have seen a kind of xenophobia developing across Europe which in fact makes political union, the ultimate aim of Europe's founding fathers as well as Jacques Delors, less likely rather than more likely. The issues that affect Europe are fundamental and should not be trivialised in terms of national caricatures which have distorted the underlying facts in people's perceptions.

In late June 2013, the *New York Times* printed a

letter written by the son of a mother of three. He told how his mother had jumped out of the kitchen window of his family's Athens apartment and alerted the world to the human cost of the financial war that has engulfed many developed countries. It took thirty years of democracy and twenty years of socialist rule for Greece to build a large and prosperous middle class, gaining its place among the countries of the developed world. This was a country that was able to host a very successful 2004 Summer Olympic Games. It has taken just three years to eradicate most of that middle class and Greece is now one step closer to being categorised as an emerging nation by the credit rating agencies.

THE FLAWS IN THE EURO PROJECT, AND WHAT IS NEEDED TO PUT THEM RIGHT

The euro project had a number of flaws. While the going was good, capital and people were encouraged to move freely across Europe as exchange rate risk was eliminated but, if anything, as Europe prospered in the euro's early years, the pace of reform in many countries slowed down. There was no pressure to implement sometimes difficult structural reforms that might lead to greater long-term productivity and growth. Looking at all of the periphery countries – not just Greece – it was obvious that the balance of payments was taking a hit. In Spain, the current account gap also widened and it is only now that domestic incomes are being squeezed and people are no longer able to buy as many foreign goods, that the current account deficit will be eliminated. Competitiveness has been lost across the board. During the boom years there was little incentive to change governance structures or the system of patronage that so discourages competition and which has been endemic in many places.

The single interest rate did not help. It allowed countries with traditionally very high interest rates before they joined the euro to grow disproportionately fast for a while as a result of the sharp cut in borrowing costs once they joined. The governments of those countries were able suddenly to borrow cheaply, in fact at the same rate as the more productive and frugal northern Europeans, as the markets priced the risk of sovereign default as the same across the whole of the eurozone. That gave some instant relief to countries that were heavily indebted, like Italy, as the cost of financing the deficits fell. But, after a while, this allowed more borrowing and the public sector grew in almost every EU country. The markets believed that there was a 'lender of last resort' or at least that no country would be allowed to default on its debts as the system was now run by the ECB. We now know that this was a mistake. At the same time, the private sector was also able to borrow a lot more cheaply, which fuelled a spending spree and an import boom. The different structures of the countries' markets, however, meant that a particular level of interest rate could in fact produce higher inflation in some countries than in others, reducing their competitiveness. In addition, the disappearance of an exchange rate risk attracted capital inflows of the sort many of these countries had not seen before, all looking for high returns and often resulting in asset bubbles. Finally, balance of payment deficits or surpluses were no longer reflected in pressures on the exchange rate. In the past, this would have been dealt with by the need to implement adjustment measures of varying intensity. Trade deficits increased in many of these periphery countries, something which the markets should have always focused on.

At the heart of the misunderstanding was how 'convergence' would work. The poorer countries would gradually see their wages come up closer to the European average and there was an expectation, finally proved in the case of Germany for example, that wages in the richest countries would stay flat or even come down fractionally. With capital flows increasing everywhere, money freely available and companies now looking at Europe as a single market for wages and costs, prices in the periphery countries rose faster than in the central and northern European ones. Their competitiveness was hit even more and the external shock of the financial crisis brought the whole house tumbling down. Replace the word 'Greece' with 'Italy' or 'Spain' on any euro 'to do' list and the list would make just as much sense.

This was the unspoken wish-list that should have accompanied the introduction of the euro:

- Reduce size of public sector
- Reduce bureaucracy

- Stop corruption
- Open up labour market
- Reduce the black market
- Reduce costs to SMEs (small and medium enterprises) and ensure funds continue to flow to deserving companies and individuals.

The problems are similar across many of the periphery countries but the intensity naturally differs. These things should have been foreseen. The fact is that they were not foreseen or at least, if discussed *sotto voce*, were not taken seriously by politicians. The eurozone was thus allowed to be created:

- Without a lender of last resort
- Without the institutional framework for occasional transfers to needy nations
- Without proper emphasis on structural reforms
- Without a firewall for crises
- Without a proper understanding of what a central bank should do during crises
- Without a long-term growth plan except completing the single market for goods and services.

Instead, what accompanied this flawed design was a Stability and Growth Pact (SGP). The pact, adopted in 1997, required all twenty-seven member states to move to a deficit of no higher than 3% of GDP and a debt-to-GDP ratio of less than 60%. The pact was in fact weakened in 2005 and has proved to be unenforceable (and it is not just Greece that has failed to meet its requirements – Germany and France have also ignored the pact in the past and ran excessive deficits for some time). It was a recipe for disaster. And we are now living through it.

2

THE ECONOMICS OF THE EURO – AND HOW THE POLITICIANS DIDN'T GET IT

Economics has a lot to say about monetary unions in general and about European monetary union (EMU) in particular. It helps to illustrate the fundamental flaws in the design of EMU as conceived in the Maastricht Treaty and it also gives us some insight into whether the eurozone was an economically coherent currency zone when it was launched – and indeed whether it is one today. Unfortunately, economics is rarely simple and is often counter-intuitive, so it's time to slow down the pace and try and explain matters as simply as possible.

Economists like to propose theories to explain the behaviour of economic agents (which includes individuals, companies and governments) and the workings of economic systems. A theory is a way of structuring arguments, assumptions and evidence and a good theory is both internally coherent and can be tested against the available evidence. In this case, the relevant theory is that of optimal currency areas, usually associated with Nobel laureate Robert Mundell. An optimal currency area in this theory is one which maximises the benefits of having a single currency relative to the costs of having a single currency.

Here's a simple example: it would make little sense for every borough in London to have its own currency with different notes, coins and exchange rates (although just down the road from me, we see an attempt to introduce a parallel currency – something rather different – in the shape of the Brixton Pound). I could be paid in the currency of the place where I work (City of Westminster) but have to pay for my bills and shopping in the currency of the place where I live (Lambeth) and even a short trip to Tate Modern, for example, would mean having to buy some third currency (in this case, Southwark). We would all be carrying huge wallets full of different notes and coins and spend a fortune in commission every time we changed money from one currency to another – or we would end up spending more time and money in the place where we lived to avoid the hassle. For an economy as highly integrated as London, a single currency facilitates movement and eliminates all these transaction costs.

However, we are not ready yet for a single currency for the entire world. This is because economics of all sizes are subject to shocks from time to time. Shocks can come in many shapes and sizes. Some can be 'nice surprises', such as when the UK discovered North Sea oil, and have the potential to make economies richer.

Other shocks are less welcome. On 11 July 2011, a munitions explosion at the Zygi naval base in Cyprus killed twelve people and also took the country's main power station out of action – reducing in a morning the productive potential of the Cypriot economy. Shocks are often asymmetric – they affect different areas in different ways and at different speeds.

Movements in exchange rates – where one currency changes in value against another – are an important safety valve in allowing economies to adjust to these shocks. A fall in a country's exchange rate relative to others means that its exports become cheaper, allowing it to export more, while imports become more expensive, which (if possible) allows imports to be substituted by domestically produced goods. So if a country is having a balance of payments problem (its export earnings are not enough to cover the cost of its imports) then a fall in its exchange rate is one way of enabling it to adjust.

So the question is, what area optimises the benefits of a single currency (primarily reduced transaction costs) compared to the disadvantages (loss of ability to adjust to shocks through varying exchange rates)? An optimal currency area would be one that shared the following characteristics:

1) Labour mobility – It needs to be easy for workers to relocate from one part of the currency area to another so that they can take advantage of opportunities elsewhere if their local economy is in the doldrums. Workers need the physical ability to move, with no

barriers such as visa requirements or work permits. There would also need to be little in the way of broader administrative barriers that discourage people from working elsewhere, such as a lack of transferability of pension or social security entitlements. There also needs to be a (relative) absence of linguistic or other cultural barriers that discourage migration.

2) Capital mobility – Similarly, money needs to be free to flow from one area to another within the currency area. This would mean the absence of any legal or administrative controls preventing or discouraging people or businesses in one part of the area from placing their savings – or investing – in another part of the currency area. But in addition to physical controls, there are subtler unwelcome ways in which capital mobility can be discouraged, for example, by governments creating hurdles to stop foreign investors buying 'their' companies.

3) Wage and price flexibility – Wages and prices within different zones of the currency area need to be able to change enough to correct for imbalances in supply and demand. So if jobs are scarce in one zone, wages there can fall to allow the employment of more people (probably accompanied by some outward migration of people if there is labour mobility and inward mobility of jobs if there is capital mobility). Legal controls on wages (or prices) or wages set through collective bargaining are not necessarily a barrier to flexibility

– what matters is how the wage levels are set and the circumstances that allow them to be varied, not the mechanism used to set them.

4) Risk-sharing mechanism – There need to be mechanisms that allow resources (money) to flow from areas doing well at a certain time to those that are failing to prosper. Tax and social security arrangements are one such mechanism as they redistribute income from the better off (tax revenues) to those less well off (social security payments). At an aggregate level, they transfer money from prosperous areas to less prosperous areas. Regional development programmes – which target deprived areas for expenditure on job creation, business support, infrastructure etc. – are another mechanism for achieving this end.

5) Convergence – The different areas within the currency area need to have business cycles that are not too far apart from each other. This is important because a single currency area has a single central bank and thus a single interest rate which applies for all of the currency area. If you have a situation where half the currency area is in recession while the other half is experiencing a boom, then any interest rate set for the area as a whole will be ineffective – it will be too high for the areas in recession (making their problem worse) and it will be too low for the booming areas (making money too cheap and inflating activity just when it needs to calm down). Note this is convergence

in terms of what makes economies move up and down over the cycle, and the timing of these movements. It is not about levels of prosperity. One half of the currency area could be twice as rich as the other and they could exist within a single currency as long as they move in sync over the business cycle (and provided the conditions above are met).

Some economists have added additional conditions, such as 'solidarity' or a sense of common purpose between the inhabitants of the currency area. These may not be strictly necessary, although it certainly makes it easier to implement a risk-sharing mechanism, such as fiscal transfers, if taxpayers within the currency area regard the welfare of others within the currency area as a source of legitimate concern – and of sufficient concern for them to be willing to finance transfer payments to help them out when these are needed. The relevance of this is obvious in the current situation, where taxpayers in Germany and other more prosperous parts of the eurozone are being asked to help meet the costs of servicing debts run up in the periphery countries: it is easier to see this happening if the people of all countries involved see themselves as Europeans with a shared destiny than it is if the argument is based entirely on national self interest.

So a particular geographical area can be identified as an optimal currency area if it possesses the five characteristics set out above. This is invariably a question of judgement, even retrospectively. These are not criteria that can be reduced to simple yes/no tests on the basis of a single number or simple condition. Let us take a hypothetical examination of whether zone A and zone B form an optimal currency area. Now consider the first characteristic, labour mobility. Suppose there are no legal barriers stopping migration between A and B and stopping inhabitants of either from working in the other. But suppose that most people in A speak French as their mother tongue and most people in B speak English. This is a potential barrier to movement. Now one must consider if there is 'enough' movement of workers in practice to facilitate A and B adjusting to shocks if they are under a single currency. How do you judge 'enough'? Well, you might compare data on actual rates of movement between A and B with data on rates of movement between areas within an optimal currency area. So if A and B above were Quebec and the rest of Canada respectively, you might compare data on mobility between these two areas with mobility within regions within the USA as a potential test of relative labour mobility.

When trying to reach an entirely professional and objective assessment, then, economists might well disagree how one decides whether a particular area is an optimal currency – as well as on whether the available evidence suggests such an area exists.

It's important to note that the development of currency areas has historically marched in step with the rise of the nation state. The ability to mint its own currency, and the right to decide legal tender within its boundaries, would often be seen as a core function of government, and thus a sign of nationhood and political independence. In practice, throughout most of the world, the currency area *is* the nation state.

Adding in the extra dimensions of politics, we now see that judgements about whether or not an area is an optimal currency area – or, more pointedly, whether two or more areas should share a single currency – are inherently political. They are also inherently subject to challenge and dispute, at a technical as well as at the political level.

So was the eurozone an optimal currency area when it was set up? An economist might answer no and that to an extent the answer remains no – and they might do this without even having to look at the data!

While the single market is meant to include freedom of movement for labour (and most of the eurozone is now part of the Schengen Agreement, which reduces border controls and other practical barriers), there are still considerable hindrances to labour mobility arising from linguistic differences and cultural preferences. There are barriers preventing the movement of people arising from differences between national social security and pension systems – still jealously guarded as the competence of nation states. Differences across countries in how qualifications obtained overseas are recognised can also distort mobility patterns.

The single market has led to the expected dismantling of capital controls, which implies free movement of capital – although, as has become clear, the financial crisis and its aftermath has led to the recognition that in itself this is not sufficient for the completion of the single market. A single currency area also requires integration of financial services – and banking in particular.

But the most obvious gap between the eurozone and an optimal currency area is the (relative) lack of a risk-sharing mechanism. The Maastricht Treaty included within the EMU a no-bail-out clause prohibiting countries from being forced to take on the financial obligations and debts of others. The European-level mechanisms for fiscal transfers are too rigid and insufficient in scale to take the strain. Contributions to the European budget are based on GDP per head, VAT receipts and a large dose of political horse-trading. Only a third of the overall EU budget is spent on the structural funds, which are in principle targeted towards poorer areas – but again with much horse-trading. And remember, the overall EU budget is only 1% of European GDP. Hence the size of these fiscal transfer mechanisms is trivial in relation to those that exist within the EU's member states.

So with all this in mind, the single currency as designed has some fundamental flaws that mean it does not meet the textbook definition of an optimal currency area. To that extent, the politicians designing it simply didn't get it.

3

GREECE MAKES HISTORY – AGAIN

There cannot be many educated people in the world who have not heard of the role the Greeks played in the creation of western civilisation. Democracy, letters, science, sport and war derive their foundation in this blessed land. But not by accident!

Greeks flourished in a land that has the globe's average temperature of about 15°C and offers most of the basic natural resources. The Hellenic tribes settled in a beautiful land of many mountains, fertile plains, deep forests, ample fresh water and a long Mediterranean coastline all around them. They enjoyed a year that offered four seasons and a huge variety of sustainable flora and fauna. A rich land provided the basics and gave the residents time for intellectual pursuits. Greece's wealth and geopolitical significance throughout the centuries made it the target of invasion and occupation by the Persians, the Romans, the Turks, the Germans and others. But it also enabled the Greeks to transfer their civilisation to faraway lands through colonisation and the creation of two empires

– the Macedonian empire created by the conquests of Alexander the Great, and the Byzantine empire created out of the eastern Roman empire – which stretched at various times to north-western Africa, the Middle East and central Asia.

Throughout history, Greece, its language and its culture prevailed. The New Testament was first written in an early form of Greek: Koine. Even Einstein and Freud used Greek for many of their scientific papers. The Olympic Games is the oldest global festival (nearly 2,800 years old).

Therefore it was no surprise that when the European powers started forming the European Economic Community, which evolved into today's European Union, Greece had to be included in the process for branding reasons. It was the first country to be granted associate member status in 1961, and it became a full member of the EEC in 1981 and, finally, a member of the eurozone in 2001. Greece's ability to meet its obligations in these consolidations was overlooked on account of its large brand value and small economic impact. Greece has consistently been a net recipient of EU funds with a net receipt of 1.3% of GDP in 2009, according to recent research from Deutsche Bank, despite structural failings that prevented their productive absorption.

This gave the Greeks the wrong impression, a belief that Europe and the world owed them a living. Their political leaders distributed these funds freely to cronies, key interest groups and the population at large to buy votes and thus sustain political dynasties. The Greek work ethic moved from 'I produce, therefore I get paid' to 'I exist, therefore I get paid'! Even worse, when a Greek looks at himself in the mirror he sees Alexander the Great and Aristotle, not Karagiozis, the popular shadow-theatre puppet character depicting the lazy, sneaky Greek under Turkish occupation.

Understanding how and why Greece found itself in its current parlous state of affairs is impossible without understanding Greece's history and political and economic systems. It is not enough to say 'Greece is corrupt' without understanding why corruption occurs and how it supports and lives off Greece's political parties.

WARS AND PEACE

It's easy to mock the Greeks with their inefficient businesses, lifetime government jobs and absurd public sector projects. But average citizens have been beleaguered for too long by forces beyond their control. Greece was invaded by the Italians and the Germans during the Second World War before being liberated by the Allies. Truman's Marshall Plan earned the US President a statue in a prominent location a short distance from the marble stadium where the Olympics were revived in 1896. But most of the funds from the plan were misdirected in funding public service jobs and creating small manufacturing plants that quickly became obsolete in the face of international competition. Unfortunately, the aid came on condition that Greece would forfeit war damage claims against the Germans, as Allied forces had a great interest in seeing Germany rebuild herself from the disastrous effects of her aggression. It included forfeiting the repayment of the gold and other assets that the occupiers 'borrowed' from the national coffers, which some estimate at between €80bn and €100bn in today's money, a multiple of Germany's contribution to Greece's bail-out.

In 1821, Greece launched similar efforts to secure foreign aid after a revolution kick-started the end of 400 years of Turkish occupation. By 1825, the rebel Greeks had succeeded in chasing away the Turks to such an extent that a provisional government was able to secure a £2m (gold) loan in London to finance its revolt and start building a national infrastructure. An upfront 'risk payment' of £1.1m was withheld by the creditors. Interest was established at 5% a year on the original amount of £2m, or £100,000 a year. British and Greek intermediaries were paid £83,500 and lawyers £13,700. Another £212,000 went to repay previous loans. Of the remainder, £156,000 went to the USA for the purchase of two frigates. Only one was delivered – and only then after the revolution was over! To turn farce into (Greek) tragedy, the frigate was promptly burned in 1831 by Greek naval hero Andreas Miaoulis, during the power struggle that ensued among the revolutionary leaders. Another £123,000 went to England to acquire six small warships. Again, only one was delivered, and again after the revolution was over. In addition, £77,200 was spent on ammunition, £37,000 as a fee to celebrated English adventurer Thomas Cochrane for taking over command of the Greek naval forces and £47,000 on 'sundry expenses'. Greece received a mere £190,000 to finance its infrastructure, which was grabbed by the revolutionary leaders to finance their civil strife. Greeks today would recognise the echoes of their current plight.

Greece began the Second World War with some success, preventing the Italian invasion of October 1940. Hitler was forced to save his militarily incompetent ally by invading Greece in April of 1941. It took the German troops three weeks to reach Athens and yet another month until they occupied Crete, where the British forces were swept aside despite the heroism and sacrifice of the soldiers. The invasion of Crete was the first large-scale paratrooper operation in history. Some historians believe that the time it took for the German forces to conquer Greece and the Balkans may have cost Germany the war, as it may have delayed the attack against Russia from spring 1941 to midsummer. Had Hitler's commanders not been obliged to divert men and materiel to crush the stubborn Greek resistance they would have enjoyed three vital months of good campaigning weather in Russia, possibly sufficient to conquer Moscow and Leningrad and alter the course of the war.

Greece suffered terribly during the war. Estimates vary but up to 700,000 people died, the vast majority being civilians killed through famine, executions, reprisals and other crimes against humanity. Among them, according to *The Columbia Guide to the Holocaust*, about 70,000 Greek Jews perished, over 90% of Greece's pre-war Jewish population. Most were from Greece's vibrant northern metropolis, Thessaloniki, which had become the home of many Spanish Jews expelled centuries earlier by the Catholic Monarchs and was the birthplace of Nicolas Sarkozy's grandfather.

At the end of the Second World War, Greece found itself part of a card game played in Yalta, between Churchill, Roosevelt and Stalin. Greece's geopolitical position was of great significance. The Balkan card was dealt to Stalin but its historic peninsula, Greece, was dealt to Churchill. Britain's wartime leader admired the fight the Greeks put up against the Axis and had accepted British casualties to defend her, committing troops to stop a Communist takeover. As ever, Churchill's oratory rings down the years: 'Today we say that Greeks fight like heroes, from now on we will say that heroes fight like Greeks.'

Peace found Greece in a continuing war: this time a destructive civil war that lasted another four years. The issue was the form of government the Greeks would choose: Communism or democracy. Families split up. Children were brought into the conflict by both sides. The Communist forces abducted children and moved them to Communist countries north of the border, to be trained to invade their homeland in later years. The royalist government set up special camps for the children of the Communist guerrillas, and some of these children were given up for adoption overseas. The award-winning film *Eleni*, based on Nicholas Gage's book, serves as a reminder of those times. The divisions that the civil war brought were only reconciled in the 1980s.

By 1950, Greece was entrenched in the western hemisphere and became a NATO member in 1952. The British, with their tradition of monarchy, insisted that Greece remained a kingdom. This eventually proved to have been a divisive decision and helped cause the political turmoil that later resulted in the regime of the Colonels of 1967 to 1974.

The years after the war were difficult years for Greece. Rebuilding a country destroyed by the Second World War while trying to reconcile a population split by the civil war was not easy. A country divided cannot move forward in tandem. There were ghosts of the past at every path. Its seven-year adventure with the junta is relatively benign compared to the much longer periods of dictatorship in Spain and Portugal, and somehow it managed.

It took two true political leaders to lead Greece to peace and prosperity. In 1955, an inspired and able leader, Constantine Karamanlis, was ushered into government, beating Communist and other leftist forces to come to power. He and his conservative party ruled for eight consecutive years. His opponent in opposition was social democrat George Papandreou. When Constantine Karamanlis came back from exile in 1974 to lead Greece in its post-junta years, the socialist opposition was led by Andreas Papandreou, George's son. Andreas Papandreou came to power in 1981 and his Pasok party has held power in Greece for all but nine years since then. And, just to confirm the dynastic nature of Greek politics, the 2004 and 2007 elections saw Kostas Karamanlis, Constantine's nephew, beat Andreas Papandreou's son, also called George Papandreou.

Constantine Karamanlis retired from politics in 1995 at the age of eighty-eight. He spent sixty years on the Greek political scene, eight years as minister, fourteen years as Prime Minister and ten years as President of the Republic. In the process he won five electoral contests. His legacy in rebuilding Greece and firmly placing it in a European trajectory is of historical proportions.

In 1981, Greece became the tenth nation to join the EEC, the very year the people voted out the conservatives for the socialists. Andreas Papandreou's legacy is different but equally important. Despite his anti-American rhetoric he kept Greece firmly in the western ranks. Under his stewardship, he redistributed wealth, creating a Greek middle class, and helped the nation heal the sores of the 1946–9 civil war by allowing former Communist fighters to return from exile. However, his wealth redistribution increased the national debt and contributed to another form of civil strife, by pitting party followers against each other for public service jobs and favours.

Kostas Simitis, successor to Andreas Papandreou as Pasok party leader, lays claim to an enviable legacy as well. In his eight years as Prime Minister (1996–2004), the German-educated technocrat applied centrist policies, saw Athens awarded the 2004 Olympic Games, ensured that Greece entered the eurozone and saw Cyprus join the EU in 2004.

STRATEGICALLY IMPORTANT BUT VULNERABLE

From the end of the Second World War, Greece was armed by its allies in recognition of its precarious location and geopolitical significance. This included making a substantial contribution to its own defence, with defence spending over most of the past thirty years of 3–5% of GDP, at a time when the nation was trying to grow and provide for its people. Communists lurked on its northern border, Crete and Cyprus served as NATO bases to keep an eye on the Suez Canal and the Middle East, while the Aegean Sea was Europe's eastern frontier. Except, ironically, on the other side of the Aegean archipelago was the Turkish coast. The armaments bought by two NATO allies, Greece and Turkey – and the military aid provided to them to fund this – faced each other instead of the non-allied borders of potential enemies.

The Ottoman Turks and Greek-speaking states (including Byzantium) have a 600-year history of wars and occupation, with the Turks occupying the Greek peninsula for 400 years. A century after the 1821 uprising that started pushing the Turks out of its territory, Greece was flourishing in Asia Minor and the Greek army was pushing for the Turkish capital of Ankara. History books on either side remind the two peoples of the evils afflicted by each other. Religious differences – Christians vs Muslims – were an additional impulse in their strife.

The beginning of the Cold War found the two nations allies under NATO for fear of the neighbouring Communist threat. It was an uncomfortable alliance. Turkey found itself cornered with a sea that seemed like a Greek lake washing on its shores. Worst of all, Cyprus, clearly adrift from the Greek mainland and 100 miles from Israel, was part of the British Commonwealth. It hosted a Turkish minority in an independent state dominated by Greek-speaking people driving on the left side of the road. Indeed, the island still hosts sovereign British military bases. Although diplomatic relations were generally cordial, disputes over territorial waters were frequent, with some Greek islands only a short swim from the Turkish mainland.

Cyprus, an EU and eurozone member that has recently applied for a bail-out itself, remains an object in the tug-of-war between Greece and Turkey over territorial control and proceeds from continental shelf (oil) exploitation rights. Turkey's claims with the 1974 invasion of Cyprus and its attempt to declare the territory conquered an independent state constitute an issue that still awaits resolution in the international forum. The bilateral issue between Greece and Turkey concerns the waters and islands that separate the two countries.

All over the world, territorial waters sovereignty extends twelve nautical miles beyond the low water mark. The same provision applies for each island, regardless of whether or not it is inhabited. Where the distance between two sovereign territories is less than twenty-four miles, a line is drawn splitting the distance. This is the case with most Greek islands along the Turkish coast on the Aegean. If Greece were to apply the international convention and prevent foreign ships from sailing in its waters, the reality of navigation would mean there are few channels of free passage in the Aegean for ships forced to stick to Turkish and international waters; a problem not only for the Turks, but also for Russian fleets coming out of the Black Sea. Turkey, as a result, refused to ratify the relevant UN convention and in 1995 the Turkish Parliament declared that if Greece, a signatory to it, applied the measure it would constitute *casus belli*: a cause for war. Greece has refrained from applying the twelve-mile convention but did something else instead: it declared a ten-mile wide territorial airspace over its islands, minus the shorter halfway lines splitting them from Turkey.

For as long as I remember, there have been daily reports in the Greek media of Turkish war planes trespassing into Greek airspace. There are probably similar reports in the Turkish media of Greek infractions into what the Turks consider their airspace. In the process, every time the Americans, the British or the French sell one of them the latest fighter plane, the other is coerced into buying its deterrent. The

USA for decades used the 10:7 rule in military aid for the two foes to maintain some sort of balance, so for every $10 of military aid credits granted to Turkey, Greece would get $7. The two nations felt extorted into overspending on arms to prevent a conflict, for the benefit of those who sold them the armaments. It is no surprise that the ex-Secretary of Defence in Greece under Pasok, Akis Tsochatzopoulos, is in jail accused of receiving millions of marks and dollars in commission and kickbacks for approving arms purchases.

Yet, suddenly, we no longer read reports of airspace violations. People residing under the flight paths the Greek Air Force took to challenge the Turkish Air Force infractions sleep quietly now. Is it because the two have given up on their claims or is it that one side cannot afford to fly any longer?

Not only can the Greek armed forces no longer afford to fly, they cannot afford to drive or sail either. Actually, they can hardly afford to operate their military equipment for lack of parts and, in many cases, the accessories and arms that make them operational. Armament contracts have many parts. You buy the hardware, then the software, then the weapons, then you train the personnel to operate them and, finally, buy the fuel to run them. Maintaining the equipment and the personnel to keep them in operational mode is another cost.

In the typically hot and dry Greek summers, it is common for there to be forest fires, caused by lightning and arsonists alike, that destroy thousands of hectares of public and private property. To combat this ongoing problem, the Greek military provide special-ised fire-fighting planes. However, at the start of the fire season in early summer 2012, less than half of the fire-fighting planes were operational due to lack of parts and maintenance.

So the one area where Greece has met auster-ity demands is in defence. The drop in expenditure has been phenomenal. Armaments deals have been postponed or cancelled altogether. Tanks, transport vehicles, war-ships and aeroplanes sit idly at their bases. Units that are part of international missions have been pulled out for lack of funds.

While lower defence spending is welcome in terms of Greece making its (reduced) ends meet, it is likely to lead to fears about future Greek–Turkish relations. Turkey is now a member of the G20 club and is being turned into a powerhouse in economic, military and even sports terms, with Istanbul one of the three cities selected by the International Olympic Committee to produce full bids to host the 2020 Olympic Games. Greeks worry that their straitened circumstances mean that it will not be long before Turkey makes a claim against Greece, and wins concessions against it, because the interna-tional community believes that Turkey matters more to the world today than Greece does.

OLYMPIC DREAMS

Negative press is not new to Greece. In the lead up to the Athens 2004 Olympic Games, Greece was castigated by the rest of the world. Given the importance often attached to the Athens Games as a cause of Greece's current financial problems, it is worth explaining just what happened, where the money went and what was done with it. While the Athens Games were certainly costly and did not deliver their full economic and social potential, they were not the complete economic and financial disaster that they are often assumed to have been.

Athens lost the 1996 Centennial Games to Atlanta despite the symbolic importance of holding them in Greece. A lack of infrastructure and vision, coupled with excessive arrogance in the bidding process, meant that Athens lost to Atlanta on the final ballot. It surprised most people therefore when the able and charismatic Gianna Angelopoulos-Daskalaki and her young bidding team put together an effort that won Greece the 2004 Games, beating Rome, Stockholm and Cape Town in the process.

The International Olympic Committee (IOC) awarded the Games to Greece in September 1997, giving it the same seven-year window as that given to London for the 2012 Olympic Games, time enough to prepare for the largest festival the world organises on a regular basis. Surprisingly, Gianna Angelopoulos-Daskalaki was cast aside in the formation of the local organising committee. It was only when the IOC pulled out a yellow card in early 2000 and threatened to take the Games away that the Prime Minister, Kostas Simitis, brought Gianna Angelopoulos-Daskalaki back and gave her carte blanche to deliver the Games on time. She did, despite the international media's insistence that the Games would be a failure. Upon closure, the media swallowed their criticism and congratulated Greece on its achievement. The London *Times* on 30 August 2004 was flushed with headlines and editorials such as 'Shed a tear for the end of this civilised Games' and 'Olympian Games – Greece gave the world two magnificent weeks of sport'.

As for the finances, the Games, by all accounts, cost Greece around €11bn; Barcelona's 1992 bill was €12bn, Beijing's 2008 bill was €32bn, while London's is expected to top out at €11bn. Atlanta in 1996 and Sydney in 2000 spent only €6.5bn and €5.6bn respectively because they already had the required infrastructure in the large open spaces in which these two cities are built.

Of the €11bn spent on Athens, €2.8bn was the operating budget; operating revenues exceeded operating expenses, leaving a surplus of around €200m. The rest, €8.2bn, was spent on much-needed infrastructural improvements, which were delivered on time, a unique 'Olympian' phenomenon when it comes to public works. Under proper planning and honest management it would have cost 30–50% less. But never mind. If it were not for the Games, Greece today would still not have a modern airport, a subway system, a ring road around the capital, north–south highways and modern telecommunications. The only thing Greece did not need, but had to purchase unexpectedly and was forced to pay for itself, was the €1.2bn for security systems and services to fend off anticipated terrorist attacks. But, before the Games opened, even these systems had helped track down 'November 17', a Greek terrorist organisation responsible for political murders and a multitude of bank robberies, plus a number of criminal activities.

Nevertheless, €8.2bn spread over seven years in a €200bn-a-year economy does not bankrupt a country. While the investment averaged 0.6% of GDP during that period, the Greek economy grew at an average pace of 4% annually. Furthermore, the Olympic Games offer the country a world stage it cannot otherwise claim – hence the huge interest by rich and poor countries alike in hosting them.

The financial assessment of the Olympic Games is not limited to sixteen days. The operational budget is structured for a break-even: IOC sponsorship and TV revenue sharing, ticket sales and other direct revenues match or exceed operational costs. The investment in infrastructure and dedicated sports facilities must therefore stimulate growth and produce future revenues that would more than recover related costs, plus improve the quality of life of the host city's citizens and, because much of the infrastructure such as the airport serves a national purpose, the citizens of the hosting country more generally. Add to this the intangible prospect of capitalising on the opportunity of being the focus of the world for two weeks. Having successfully staged the biggest festival in the world certainly adds brand value to your homeland!

These days, the IOC is very serious about awarding the Games to cities that prove the positive impact of the Olympic legacy to their people. A candidate city needs to convincingly demonstrate how the Olympics will benefit its community once the Games are over. Barcelona opened the city to the sea; it used the world stage to turn the Catalan capital into one of the top congress and convention destinations in the world today. Beijing was turned into a functional city and showed the world that China was ready for global business. London has revamped its neglected east-end neighbourhoods. Athens benefited from infrastructure, but built some unnecessary white elephants, still standing idle today. Because the international media spent seven years criticising its preparations, however, Greece did fail to capitalise on its global exposure.

Once Greece delivered the most successful Games to that date, all spoke of the Greek method of delivery. It resembled the *syrtaki* dance – starting slowly, it gradually builds to a crescendo of vivid synchronised dancing and jumping within a circle. Not much different from a runner who comes from behind with a strong finish, as Dame Kelly Holmes did twice in Athens to win gold.

Maybe this is what we are seeing today. Greece initially cut back spending aggressively and managed to reduce the budget deficit substantially early on in the bail-out process. However, it made a slow start in complying with many other aspects of the terms attached to its bail-out, in particular the pace of reforms, cutting out bureaucracy and red tape, opening up its markets and reducing an oversized public sector. The apparent lack of good faith and the sheer incompetence seen in that period have led to much frustration on the part of its European partners and the IMF. Now that the yellow card has been issued by the troika and the talk of exiting the euro brings back memories of losing the Games, maybe the Greeks will get their act together again and pull off the same miracle they managed in 2004.

4

GREECE: THE RICHEST NATION IN THE WORLD TO PRODUCE NOTHING?

In an article entitled 'Greece vs. the Rest', the *New Yorker* magazine described the country as 'the richest nation in the world that produces nothing!' Now even the harshest critic of Greece would say this is obviously untrue – Greece has clearly shown itself to be highly active in the production of red tape, bureaucratic inertia and ineffective politicians on the make! But this is not the whole story. While the political, administrative and judicial systems in Greece are dysfunctional, there is potential in sectors of the economy which could be harnessed to drive a more prosperous future for Greece.

GREECE – THE CLIENTELIST STATE

When you see that in order to produce, you need to obtain permission from men who produce nothing; when you see that money is flowing to those who deal, not in goods, but in favors; when you see that men get richer by graft and by pull than by work, and your laws don't protect you against them, but protect them against you; when you see corruption being rewarded and honesty becoming a self-sacrifice; you may know that your society is doomed.

Ayn Rand

Ayn Rand went to America from her native Russia soon after the Bolshevik takeover, having witnessed the dead hand of unproductive bureaucracy suck the energy out of economic endeavour. Her comments are tailor-made for Greece where a whole science of non-productive employment was shaped. Consider the following anecdote – quite possibly an urban myth but all too plausible:

Some years ago a small rural town in Spain twinned with a similar town in Greece. The Mayor of the Greek town visited the Spanish town. When he saw the palatial mansion belonging to the Spanish Mayor he wondered how he could afford such a house.

The Spaniard said, 'You see that bridge over there? The EU gave us a grant to build a two-lane bridge, but by building a single-lane bridge with traffic lights at either end this house could be built.'

The following year the Spaniard visited the Greek town. He was simply amazed at the Greek Mayor's house, gold taps, marble floors; it was marvellous. When he asked how this could be afforded the Greek said:

'You see that bridge over there?'

The Spaniard replied, 'No.'

Greece is an example of what political scientists would term a 'clientelist state'. It is one characterised by exchanges of favours between politicians and interest groups, which could be friends and relatives of the politicians, businesses, other organised interest groups or trade unions. Clientelism can exist both in democracies and in dictatorships, and exchanges of favours can be open (party contributions rewarded with prestige appointments, as arguably happens when a newly elected US President rewards campaign contributors with jobs in the administration or plum ambassadorships) or under the table (bribes to secure public contracts).

Louka Katseli, who became a minister in 2009 as part of George Papandreou's Pasok administration, referred to the concept of 'extractive institutions', as discussed in Daron Acemoglu and James Robinson's book *Why Nations Fail: The Origins of Power, Prosperity and Poverty*. In her view, the 'closed circuit' relationship between politicians, business, the media and the banks comprised a set of extractive institutions, a system bent on creating profit or surplus for favoured interest groups rather than promoting positive restructuring of the economy.

Whichever terminology we use, the story is the same. Greece has a very good system for sharing the spoils of the electorate's efforts – the problem is the system appears much less interested in and is much less effective at making the electorate as a whole richer.

MONEY BUYS POWER

Political parties in Greece raise their funds from a variety of sources: 1) annual state endowments based on the number of MP seats controlled, which the Parliament votes in; 2) bank loans taken out against future state endowments (which of course will be voted for by future MPs, so we can see that they are likely to be regarded as very low risk, plus of course giving the banks some extra leverage over the political parties); 3) party members' contributions; and 4) undeclared corporate contributions (which could be anything from bribes to commission for favours rendered and extortion).

Over the past ten years, New Democracy has benefited from state endowments to the tune of €271m and Pasok to the tune of €254m, or an average of €26m a year each. In addition to that, they jointly owe an additional €260m to the banks. That brings the average expenditures of each to close to €40m a year, before contributions over and under the table by political clients. And it's not just the bigger parties. KKE (the unreformed Communist Party) was endowed with €64m and Syriza with €48m during the same ten-year period.

In comparison, take a look at the UK, a country five times larger in terms of population. From 2008 to 2012, the latest Electoral Commission analyses of statements of account show that the Conservative Party had an average income of about £38m and the Labour Party had an average income of about £29m.

Unlike the major parties in the UK, who are aiming to reduce their costs and improve their overall financial position, running up debts to third parties was of no concern to New Democracy and Pasok. So what if they owe huge amounts to the advertising agencies that undertook their political campaigns? They would be rewarded in due time with overpriced campaigns for the state or for state-owned companies, which would recover their costs and missed profits. 'Undisclosed' contributors would also receive relevant benefits. One example that has come to light as a result of a parliamentary investigation is that for many years Siemens apparently made payments to politicians from both major parties to secure lucrative contracts. Indeed, the network of businesses and media owners behind these arrangements is often described as the 'national contractors'. However, Parliament has now shown itself reluctant to accord the same endowments to the parties, reducing them by 30–50%. This means the main parties are effectively bankrupt – just like the country, some would say! One of the rumours circulating in Athens in the summer of 2012 was that one of the parties had not paid salaries to its employees in months and owed many months' back rent to the landlord of the party headquarters. The fear must be that, because of their difficult financial position and with less support from the state, political parties when in government will need to be even more aggressive in trading party contributions for favours over choice of contractors, for example.

The interest groups tied into this system range widely. For example, politics and football are synonymous in Greece. They evoke the same passion around any private or public gathering. Again, it is argued that existing or aspiring national and regional contractors buy teams to hold the central or regional government hostage to their agendas. They present politicians with millions or thousands of fans who will swing for or against them, depending on how they treat the club or the club owner. If true then it is no surprise that tax debts to the state are summarily forgiven on the eve of elections or that owners' companies are awarded government contracts. The biggest names in the Greek business élite have at one time been owners of popular football clubs ostensibly to leverage their demands.

Even the Greek Orthodox Church plays its part. Religion is not so much a belief among Greeks as it is part of their culture: a unifying force with links to others of similar faith in the Balkans and the old Soviet republics. The best way to describe the coexistence of the Greek state with the Greek Church is the letter sent to the Prime Minister, related ministers and foreign ambassadors by the Greek Archbishop Hieronymus, in late July 2012 concerning taxation of the Church. In this, the archbishop claimed that the issue of Church taxation had been distorted. He referred to an 1833 agreement between the newly founded nation of Greece and the Orthodox Church, which handed over two-thirds of the church's real estate holdings to the country to give it land holdings. Over the years, 96% of the Church's urban and rural holdings were turned over to the state. In return, the state does not tax the remaining holdings of the Church and pays the salaries and benefits of the clergy that the Church hires. 'Render unto Caesar that which is Caesar's' is an old biblical injunction. In Greece, the taxpayer provides massive financial support for the Church, which manages to avoid paying any direct tax.

IT'S A SMALL WORLD

As we have seen, Greece's politics is virtually a two-family affair. Like the Montagues and Capulets in Shakespeare's Verona, the two gentlemen of Athens, Mr Papandreou and Mr Karamanlis, held sway over the nation. Families are at the heart of Greek life but republican politics requires new blood and a regular infusion of new ideas and personalities. This attribute of modern democracy failed to emerge. In the 2004 and 2007 national elections, George Papandreou, Andreas's son and George's grandson, lost to Kostas Karamanlis, the nephew of Constantine who spent twenty years as Prime Minister and as President of the Republic. In the face of the oncoming economic crisis, Kostas stood down in 2009, opening the door of the New Democracy party leadership to Antonis Samaras. George, still fighting, came to power in a landslide victory in October 2009 over Antonis.

George Papandreou and Kostas Karamanlis were both propelled to the leadership by their parties' political strategists. Their value to the party was their name, deferring to the feats of their ancestors – this was believed to attract voters and strengthen loyalty to the party. It may also have had the not entirely unwelcome consequence of making it less likely that the party leaders would make a break from, or dissociate themselves from, the actions of their predecessors and those that aided, funded and benefited from them.

The political élite more generally come from a relatively small and closely knit circle. Antonis Samaras, who lost the election in 2009 but is now Prime Minister, was a student at Athens College, the US-endowed ten-year (fourth to thirteenth grade) secondary school for the Greek élite also attended by George Papandreou and his father before that. They both ended up attending universities in the same Massachusetts town and George Papandreou and Antonis Samaras were roommates at Amherst College.

While at the highly politicised Athens College, Antonis's classmate Nicos Bistis (who was on the championship volleyball team that my brother captained) was the political leader of the school – not Antonis. Nicos, an activist against the junta, later joined leftist parties and eventually became a minister under Pasok, and is now a member of the Democratic Left party (DIMAR). Louka Katseli, who became a minister under George Papandreou, also attended university (Smith College) in the same Massachusetts neighbourhood.

In the last fifty years, a Karamanlis has been in a ruling position for twenty of those and a Papandreou for thirteen. In between, another political family came to prominence. Its leader, Constantine Mitsotakis, a Cretan, caused the collapse of George (grandfather) Papandreou's government by leading a group of deputies across party lines to the conservative camp. He ended up becoming Prime Minister as leader of New Democracy in 1990, only to see his government collapse when his then Foreign Minister, Antonis Samaras, deserted him in a vote of confidence procedure. His daughter, Dora Bakoyiannis, Mayor of Athens, challenged Samaras for the New Democracy leadership in 2009 and, upon losing, formed her own party, although she is back with Samaras and New Democracy today.

Political dynasties are not unique to Greece; they exist in other democracies. We have seen three generations of Kennedys in the USA, like the Papandreous, and in India the Congress Party machine is preparing the ground for a fourth generation of the Nehru–Gandhi line to take power. Nature (and nurture) to one side, a family name can be a very handy way of gaining attention from the voters and communicating a certain brand value. However, its prevalence in Greece, and the very close familial and other ties connecting the political élite, create the conditions for – even if they do not necessarily guarantee – the clientelism observed in the Greek political class.

A SYSTEM THAT ENCOURAGES EVERYONE TO AVOID THEIR RESPONSIBILITIES

Prosperity requires a fair judicial system, steady and predictable taxation, and an effective bureaucracy. Greece is seen as lacking all of these. Transparency International publishes a Corruption Perceptions Index, measuring perceived public sector corruption based on data from a range of sources. The 2011 ranking showed Greece in joint eightieth position alongside El Salvador, Morocco, Peru and Thailand, and hence the most corrupt EU member state included in these rankings.

The management of public revenues is a sign of good governance. If the people are taxed equitably, pay their taxes for fear of the judicial system and benefit from their use, society will prosper. In Greece, according to credible surveys, 85% of the taxes are used to pay for public sector jobs and wasteful expenses. The construction of a highway can cost six times more than one built to the same standards in any other EU country. The taxation system itself is unfair, paranoid and contradictory, and it changes every few months. In one year, 2011, it was changed eleven times with different taxation systems announced again and again. It is impossible for even the employees in the tax offices to learn and understand all these changes. Citizens feel like victims of gang extortion: they must pay because the Greek state will harm them if they do not, while at the same time they know that their money ends up in the pockets of politicians and their friends. The people must save money in order to bribe the taxman that will audit them as well as the physician who will operate on them or a member of their family. As a result, people feel that tax evasion is both logical and morally legitimate and taxes collected in Greece amount to a mere 7.3% of GDP, as opposed to an 11% average for the EU.

Tax evasion results in a large black economy, which in Greece is estimated at around a quarter of GDP. While any such estimate is bound to be unreliable by its nature, that is on the face of it €52bn of untaxed economic activity. The troika's insistence on raising the VAT rate to 23% and bringing goods and services once rated at less than 10% under this higher rate has earned Greece another last place in the EU rankings – Greece has managed to collect only 37% of the VAT receipts it had budgeted for 2010. In an effort to highlight the ineffectiveness of tax laws forced upon the population by Greece's lenders, my brother sent a note to the Task Force for Greece, the agency run by Horst Reichenbach and set up by the troika to guide the country's governance, concerning his experience with his plumber. Presented with a €600 bill for a broken pipes repair, he was confronted with the dilemma of paying it in cash or adding 23% VAT and assuming an additional cost of €138 to be 'donated' to the government for 'public services' or debt repayment. As new tax regulations no longer deemed house repairs as tax deductible, the incentive would have been to pay under the table. The government would thus lose not only the VAT but also tax on the plumber's undeclared income. In response, a Task Force executive replied stating, rather like a recent UK Treasury minister, that he should force a legal transaction on the basis of 'principle', disregarding the lack of incentive to do so!

A lack of willingness to pay taxes is part of the problem – but only part. The Greek state is hopelessly ineffective at tackling tax evasion. By mid-2013, tax and customs infractions over the past years resulted in irrevocable court decisions amounting to a staggering €14.4bn in back taxes and fines, of which only €742.3m or 5.14% of the total amount owing had been paid. Collecting five cents of every euro owed is not a record to be proud of, especially when 100% collection would, for at least one year, have bridged much of the gap in the overall government finances.

However, the citizens feel that the government itself is untrustworthy in fulfilling its obligations. It still owes some €8.5bn to domestic suppliers, strangling construction companies, manufacturers of pharmaceuticals, consultancies and others. In a recent incident, authorities arrested, with great fanfare, the CEO of a major construction company in a public–private partnership highway venture for unpaid taxes – when the government apparently owed the same company six times this amount!

Governments have also shown themselves to be mercurial and inconsistent, properties that damage confidence and make investment a gamble. A few years ago, the government of Kostas Karamanlis significantly lowered the taxation of cars, particularly the larger-engined ones, while offering cash bonuses to those who scrapped their old vehicles. This measure was meant to clear Greek roads and city streets of the polluting clunkers still in circulation. Car sales doubled in a euphoric run to auto dealers, while the country's balance of payments suffered since Greece does not manufacture automobiles. A few years later, the government turned around and retaxed the same car categories even more severely, while seeking additional income tax from owners who spent more on a car than they had declared as income. The effects were so disastrous that owners were forced to withdraw them from circulation, their resale value reduced to scrap for lack of second-hand buyers. Half the car dealerships have since closed down.

WHAT DOES GREECE MAKE?

Q: 'What's a Greek Urn?'
A: 'Not a lot!'
Old music hall joke as adapted by Morecambe and Wise

Modern Greece is thought by many observers to be quite like *Zorba the Greek*, the award-winning 1964 film by Michalis Kakoyannis, starring Anthony Quinn, Alan Bates and Irene Pappas, based on Nikos Kazantzakis's novel. The story centres on the adventures of two partners poised to build a mine near a remote village in Crete. A project that would make them rich and the village prosper was not altogether embraced by the suspicious locals who saw their tranquil lives upended. After a long and arduous effort, full of distracting conflicts, love and drama, the mine was completed. But with the whole village present to witness its inauguration, it collapses and self-destructs! Unperturbed, the hero exclaims, 'Life is all about unbuckling your belt and looking for trouble.' He then leads his partner, shoulder to shoulder, in the dance that has been Greece's trademark ever since: the slow-starting but gradually accelerating *syrtaki* referred to earlier and known the world over.

It has been years since anyone said anything positive about the Greek economy. But there's a local saying that when a spring is pressed down hardest, it can spring back the fastest.
New York Times, 3 July 2012

So the question is: what is Greece truly known for in terms of products and services consumed around the world? How can it earn a living (in or out of the euro)?

In terms of statistics, Figure 4.1 presents a breakdown of gross value added (a measure of business sector output) by broad industrial sector, and compares Greece with the eurozone as a whole. The Greek economy has a larger agricultural sector than the average, although still accounting for just 3.3% of total gross value added. The big difference from other countries is that trade, transport and communication services account for a bigger share of value added – which will include shipping and many tourism-related services – whereas Greece has an under-representation in business and financial services.

FIGURE 4.1: SECTOR BREAKDOWN OF GROSS VALUE ADDED, 2010

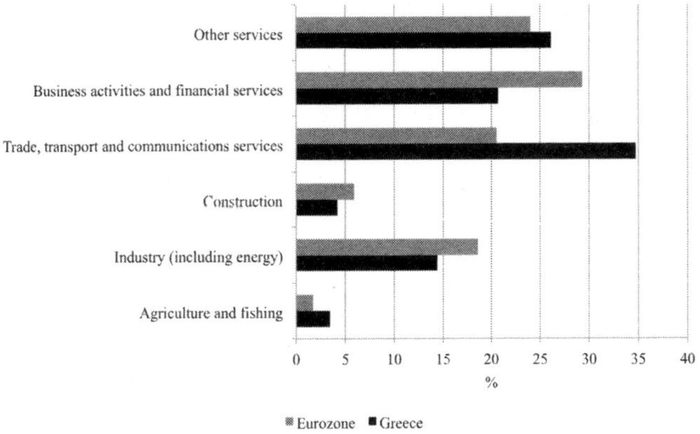

Source: Eurostat.

TOURISM AND CULTURE

In a recent survey among *Traveller* magazine readers, Greece was second in terms of countries associated with island vacations, after the Maldives. However, the country's character has changed as Greeks have tried to capitalise on their country's history, beautiful landscape and inviting climate. They went about it in a disorganised, ruinous, overpriced, brash manner as they exploited its assets. 'A room with a sea view and a nearby ruin' has been the country's unchanged tourism strategy since the 1960s, when the world discovered it as a tourist destination.

Quickly, the country was left behind as neighbouring states like Turkey and Croatia developed strategies that bring in the numbers and revenues. Turkey receives almost triple the number of visitors Greece does today, while the likes of Italy and Spain continue to increase their numbers. It all boils down to the ultimate consumer criterion: value for money. And Greece has been lagging behind in this department for years. If it isn't violent political demonstrations that scare people away from Athens, it is the price of goods and services on the islands.

It does seem, however, that shop owners have finally begun to realise that price competitiveness does matter. There have been reports of significant cuts in the cost of lodging, food and other services on various islands to attract business. At the end of the summer season in 2013 foreign tourist numbers were 10% higher than the previous year with a further two million expected in the early autumn season when the sun still shines on Greece. The Aegean is home to the warmest autumn sea in the northern hemisphere and Greece's USP remains its extraordinary weather and endless coastlines. Visitor tourism receipts in 2013 are estimated to come in at a healthy €11.5bn. But this is still a low €650 per capita compared to Turkey and Spain, and Greece's planning, legal and administrative hurdles prevent mass or luxury tourism developing. In addition, domestic Greek tourism is likely to have dropped by another 10–15% in 2013, or more than half since the pre-crisis numbers, as Greeks skip or shorten their holiday period. Newspapers have carried reports alleging increasing tax evasion in many popular tourist destinations. Greeks love taking vacations in their own country but the EU troika's austerity policies and slashing of incomes have reduced internal demand for vacations.

AGRICULTURE

Flying over Greece one is struck by the vast area of the country that is mountainous and/or covered by forests. Only a third of the land, at best, can be cultivated. And yet the Greeks still produce a variety of agricultural products for domestic production and export, some unique in quality like olives (and olive oil), fruits (e.g. peaches, citrus and grapes), vegetables (beans and tomatoes) and cash crops, like tobacco and cotton. But little value has been added to Greek agricultural produce, with it tending to be shipped in its raw form. New crops of higher value have been added to the agricultural mix over the years, like avocado, broccoli, saffron, kiwis and so on, which benefit from the Greek soil and climate conditions. There has also been a huge upgrade in wine production by crossing imported vine varieties with the indigenous. But Greece has a lot further to go and would benefit from an agricultural revolution and greater consolidation in the sector, something which has escaped it in the past.

Up until it joined the Common Agricultural Policy (CAP) system, Greece was self-sufficient and had an agricultural trade surplus, importing mostly beef and milk products (the terrain supports mostly goats and sheep but few cows). Consumption was seasonal. But then markets opened up and it was easy to import products for year-round consumption. Production suffered. Various reports suggest that in the absence of proper control mechanisms, the subsidies flowing in for new tractors and technology were misspent. The year 2011 saw a flurry of articles on whether Larissa, the agricultural capital of Greece, had the highest per capita concentration of Porsche Cayennes in the world!

Greece started losing its culinary identity and there were serious marketing failures. Feta cheese, for example, which has been mandated by an EU ruling as coming exclusively from Greece, has been imitated all over the world, losing Greece the global market in feta-style cheese. The same thing happened when Greek yogurt, a significant export product, invaded the UK and US markets. The Greek producers' inability to capitalise on new markets created an industry for imitation by the dairy giants, re-branding theirs as 'Greek-Style Yogurt', limiting the original product to a decreasing (30%) market share.

Greece also produces high-quality olive oil, mostly of the coveted 'extra virgin' quality. But, again, it markets it very poorly. It exports in branded bottles only 10,000 tons of the 200,000-plus tons it exports in its raw form. Italy, which imports most of Greece's olive oil in bulk and then bottles it as Italian produce, and Spain, which accounts for half the world's olive oil production, now dominate the world's retail markets. The Greeks must improve their marketing if they are to add value to their goods.

FISHERIES

Small fishing fleets and disastrous fishing practices have depleted the fish population of Greece's seas. So has the appearance of industrial trawlers from Portugal, Spain and Turkey, fishing on the fringe of Greece's exclusive territorial waters. But, in recent years, entrepreneurs have created fisheries along the coast and islands. Greece today produces around 50% of the farmed Mediterranean fish consumed in the EU, and has increased its global share with technological advances. It comes as no surprise that international investment funds have recently been showing interest in investing in Greek fisheries.

SHIPPING

From the trading and battle ships of ancient Greece to the commercial success of the nineteenth-century naval families, Greece has always had a powerful shipping fleet.

When Greek ship-owners, led by the legendary Aristotle Onassis, negotiated the sale of a hundred obsolete US-built, liberty-class, single-hull, all-purpose freighters to them by the US government with financial guarantees by the Greek state, the Greeks became the predominant shipping power post-Second World War. Having gained the trust of financiers through their shipbuilding prowess and business acumen, they enlarged their fleets to meet the world's shipping demands and the Greeks are now the proud owners of the largest merchant shipping fleet in the world with a 16% share. No other nation, besides Japan, even comes close.

For the past few years Greeks have accounted for nearly 50% of new orders to the shipyards of South Korea and China. The Greek-owned fleet is today one of the newest and safest in the world. And no nation has more shipping companies listed in the US stock markets than Greece. Shipping receipts are the second largest item in foreign exchange earnings after tourism. But the economic downturn has affected the sector negatively across all areas of business with it becoming the focus of attention given the tax concessions it enjoys. As a counter it argues that it has contributed some €175bn into the Greek economy between 2000 and 2010, something which would not have happened if those concessions were not applicable.

ENERGY

Greece is blessed with more than 300 days of sun and in many places steady 20–40 miles an hour seasonal winds. Wind power can be generated through offshore installations along the hundreds of uninhabited islands in the Greek archipelago. Recently, calls for tender to explore offshore drilling for natural gas brought eight respectable multinationals applying for exploration licences. Will the Greek bureaucracy allow entrepreneurs to bring to market Greece's energy resources? Or will the Greek politicians and civil servants fix deals behind closed government doors? In the past, these 'arrangements', as they are known in Greece, are believed to have distorted open transparent market competition.

But has Greece gone too green too fast? Driving around Greece in the summer of 2013 I was struck by extensive solar panels dispersed among the fertile agricultural fields of central Greece and wind farms on the ridges of the country's hills and mountains. Greece, facing the 20% EU target on energy from renewable resources by 2020, embarked on a policy of incentives to achieve it. Greece is not the only country in the EU to have established ill-thought strategies, at least in the short term, to adhere to the EU directive. Greece is among the largest producers of the highly pollutant but cheap lignite (soft carbon) used to power its electrical plants. Electricity produced by (imported) natural gas is reported to cost twice as much as that by lignite and subsidies and price guarantees for the fledging solar and wind power industry brings the cost of energy from renewable resources to some three times that again. By July 2013, lignite was the source of 39% of the electricity produced in Greece, with renewable resources accounting for 16% and gas for 28%. The rest came from oil. It is true that similar things are going on across Europe but it is arguable whether Greece can afford the substantial increase in energy costs to Greek industry at a time when the country needs desperately to improve its international competitiveness.

On the positive side, the future may reveal underwater wealth that could make Greece (and Cyprus) major providers of natural gas. This has been rumoured for a while but seismic tests have now hinted of significant finds. Cyprus has already assigned exploration rights among claims (though so far so unproven) that the Greece–Cyprus–Israel natural seabed gas reserves can provide 50% of the EU's energy needs for the next thirty years! But energy company Noble Energy is drilling in Cyprus's 200-mile continental shelf and the Greek government is expected to award drilling contracts for the Ionian and Patras underwater fields by September 2013. Results are expected as early as 2014. Is there hope after all?

INDUSTRY

With an internal market that does not provide for economies of scale, export markets had to be opened. But that couldn't happen in an introverted economy which turned down Toyota's 1980s proposal to build its main European plant in Volos, central Greece, ostensibly in order to protect an industrialist who had invested in assembling a jeep-like vehicle with a Citroën engine – it was called the Pony but went slower than the four-legged variety.

The only 'Made in Greece' inscription that one could find while abroad was on clothes and manual shavers. The textile industry priced itself out of the international markets long ago. Somehow, under the management of its initial owner, BIC still makes a couple of lines of its blade shavers in Greece.

CONSTRUCTION

This is one of the country's largest sectors and it has been the locomotive for growth since the 1950s due to the need for public works and dwellings to house the increasing number of people flocking to the cities. Whole neighbourhoods of small detached homes with little gardens, like the one I was born in, were turned into wall-to-wall, five-storey apartment blocks, like the one I grew up in. A quasi-barter deal was invented where the owner would grant his property to a developer against a 40–50% ownership of the finished building. Financing, in those days, came through pre-sales in cash and promissory notes. In later years, banks fuelled further growth – until the real estate bubble burst. But in all cases, no one had to declare the source of their income to acquire real estate. This meant that somebody with €20,000 in annual income could find himself or herself outright owner of a €200,000 home, without any questions being asked. Attempts by the government to impose a real estate tax to recover part of the untaxed or laundered income that went towards buying these properties have mostly backfired.

It was an attractive deal for all and new developments are still structured on a similar foundation. The new dwellings offered amenities and comforts most families didn't have in the first half of the twentieth century. This included running water, central sewerage and electricity. But the result was not necessarily attractive, as it turned what today would be classified as historic districts into nondescript apartment blocks. Once the new owners moved further up in terms of income brackets, they built a holiday home and, later, renovated their ancestral home in the village of their origin. Often, their holiday or primary home was built on unzoned, forested, state-owned land. Developers are thought to be responsible for causing forest fires and, immediately after, putting up the skeletons of residences to be sold later in the knowledge that retroactive legalisation would continue to be used as a traditional tool by those in power to attract political support. The defoliation of the Athens basin forests of Pendeli, Parnitha and Hymettus is a reminder of residential development gone awry.

Greece is the only EU member that does not have a complete land register. The funding to establish it came from the EU twenty years ago and all of it was spent before much progress was made in creating a credible, electronic register. It is no surprise that only 33% of the state land earmarked for privatisation is free from third-party violations and claims. The century-old rule that if you occupy a premises for twenty years, with no one complaining, then you have a legal claim for it seemed to suit the agenda of politicians and their patrons.

Slowly, Greeks moved to the top of the home ownership league table, hitting a rate of 80%. Actually, the average Greek owns 2.2 properties, even if he or she is renting their current dwelling. All this construction activity led to an industry of architects, engineers and construction specialists. Greece is one of the top producers of cement in the world. Steel, aluminium and other building materials in raw or manufactured form constitute main exports for Greece.

Public infrastructure financed by the EU created, through mergers, an industry of large construction firms that built roads, subways, ports and plants not only in Greece but also in the Balkans and the Middle East. However, as ever, collusion with government caused budget and timeline overruns, depleting funds at great cost to the people. One still wonders how a national government under supervision and monitoring from Brussels could build a road at a cost six times that of Germany's. How much went to kickbacks (contractors to politicians), how much to unreasonable expropriation costs (government to voters) and how much to the actual cost of the project (social benefits)? This is a prime illustration of how corruption works to the detriment of the people and the country. Ironically, the lowest overruns were recorded in the rush to complete the Olympic projects before the Athens 2004 Summer Games.

DO WE LAUGH OR CRY?

What irritates those called upon to help Greece are the deficiencies, anomalies and plain madness in the way it is structured and governed. The worst examples find their way to the international media – and to Berlin, Brussels and the troika. Here are some:

- As of the end of August 2013, in asked-for but unpaid back taxes and fines for non-payment, private individuals owed the state a record €21.5bn and companies €38.5bn. And this was in addition to the tens of billions of euros missing due to tax evasion.

- Of Greece's forecast revenues from its privatisation programme, 50% revolve around state-owned land. But apparently when assessors went to inspect a particular 2,000 metric acre parcel in the Peloponnese, they found that only 120 were free and clear, as the rest had been trespassed and illegally 'privatised' by the same locals who object to the sell-off of state assets.

- Six Airbuses, each eight years old and in full flying capacity, were put up for sale by state-owned Olympic Airways in 2007 for an assessed price of €40m each. Unionised Olympic Airways employees objected to their sale because it cut into jobs. As time went by, their value dropped to less than 75% of their acquired value. Greek law forbids the sale of state property at less than 75% of its acquired value. In July 2012 they were sold for scrap.

- Figures provided to me suggest that in the state-owned national railways, 1,987 employees get an extra monthly stipend of €420 for washing their hands. An extra €310 goes to 1,790 employees of the national Trolley Bus Company for coming to work on time and an additional 329 get €1,120 in 'hardship' remuneration for working under an electrical antenna. For transporting files from one place to the other, 6,800 public servants get an extra €290 a month, while those on board coastguard vessels get an additional €840 'propeller' bonus a month. Among the drivers of the state bus company, those that actually warm up their buses before hitting the streets are rewarded with an additional €690 a month. And the 657 employees of the state electric company who know how to send a fax get an extra €870 a month.

- There are 580 hardship professions that have been created by decree over the years, allowing those in them to retire early with full benefits because of the particular hardships of their professions. These include everything from tuba players to hairdressers – and 400 still remain in place. It is only now, at the moment of crisis, that the government has finally summoned the nerve to tackle this anomaly.

- Truckers, taxi drivers and pall bearers are among the dozens of professions protected for decades by a freeze in licences for new entrants. The protection of specific professions earns votes but adds significantly to costs by stifling competition. A loaded truck going from point A to point B cannot bring back goods from B to A. It returns empty, while another loaded truck drives from B to A and empty from A to B. This, in effect, has doubled the cost of commercial transport in Greece. And pall bearers get a fixed €600 each time they carry a casket from the cemetery's church to the grave. No wonder each cemetery has a family that has profited from such exclusivity for generations.

- There are so many absurd regulations to adhere to, and permits to obtain, in order to open a gymnasium that the same government that created them voted an exemption to the rules in order to open one for Members of Parliament!

Yes, do we laugh or cry? How does a system so broken reform itself? Can it even reform itself? When you see such examples you can understand why officials from the troika, who have generally made their career in relatively efficient and well-ordered administrations, despair about Greece reforming itself. Indeed, some of the Greek politicians I spoke to in researching this book had a deep sense of pessimism about the ability of Greece to change. Even if the politicians were willing to take tough decisions, they had no effective means of ensuring that the policies they approved (some very painful politically) would ever be turned into action. Yet without wide-ranging reform of the working of its political, administrative and judicial systems Greece will find it difficult to emerge from its current plight.

5

GREECE IN CRISIS

On 31 December 1998, the conversion rates between the euro and the currencies of the participating member states were irrevocably fixed. On 1 January 1999, the euro was introduced and the eurosystem, comprising the European Central Bank (ECB) and the national central banks of the eurozone member states, took over responsibility for monetary policy in the new euro area. This was the beginning of a transitional period that was to last three years andend with the introduction of euro banknotes and coins, and the withdrawal of national banknotes and coins. Eleven European countries started using the euro as a step towards economic union: Austria, Finland, France, Belgium, Germany, Ireland, Italy, Luxembourg, the Netherlands, Portugal and Spain. In 2000, the European Council decided that Greece fulfilled the necessary conditions for the adoption of the single currency, and the country joined the euro area on 1 January 2001.

The then President of the ECB, Wim Duisenberg, warned that Greece still had a lot of work to do to improve its economy and bring inflation under control. Greece was not included in the eurozone in 1999 as it failed to meet the economic criteria set down in the Maastricht Treaty. When Greece's application to join the euro came back before the European Council in spring 2000, it was not an open-and-shut decision. The 'Convergence 2000' report prepared by the ECB did not make a recommendation on whether or not Greece should be admitted – it presented the ECB's assessment of the evidence and left that decision to the Council. The report makes interesting reading.

FIGURE 5.1: INFLATION IN GREECE BEFORE AND AFTER ENTRY TO THE EURO

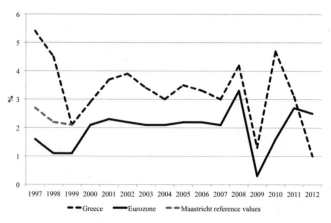

Source: Eurostat and European Central Bank 'Convergence Report 2000' for Maastricht reference values. The inflation measure used is the Harmonised Index of Consumer Prices.

One of the Maastricht entry criteria was that inflation – as measured by the Harmonised Index of

Consumer Prices – should be within 1.5% of the average of the three states with the lowest inflation rate. Figure 5.1 shows that, at the time, Greece just met this criterion, although before then and since then its inflation rate has consistently been above the eurozone average.

However, the ECB convergence report mentions various price freezes and 'gentlemen's agreements' that had been put in place to keep prices low, and speculates whether these are sustainable.

FIGURE 5.2: GREEK GOVERNMENT FINANCES SINCE JOINING THE EUROZONE

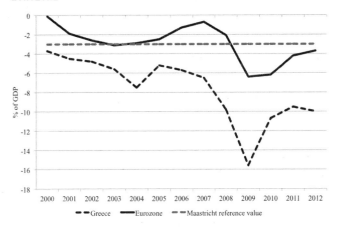

Source: Eurostat. Negative value indicates a budget deficit.

Another criterion for euro membership was that the budget deficit had to be kept to 3% of GDP or less. To achieve this, the Greek government had to adopt a tough austerity programme, making deep cuts in public spending, which it clearly did. However, at this time there was much concern about the data on the budget deficit and whether they had been falsified or manipulated in order to get the measured deficit down below 3%. Part of that debate concerned the national accounting standard used and whether the move from an old European standard to a new European standard made a difference. Figure 5.2 shows that, since euro entry, Greece has failed in most years to get its budget deficit anywhere near the 3% Maastricht criterion.

FIGURE 5.3: GREEK DEBT-TO-GDP RATIO BEFORE AND AFTER ENTRY TO THE EUROZONE

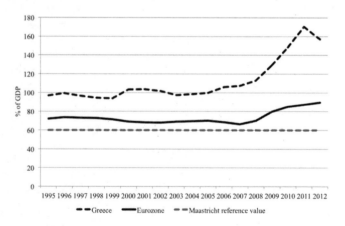

Source: Eurostat. General government gross debt.

A third Maastricht criterion concerned the ratio of public debt to GDP. The reference value was 60%. Figure 5.3 shows that Greece was nowhere near this.

However, it had been recognised that this was not a binding constraint – Belgium and Italy had been admitted to the euro with debt ratios much higher than 60% – and what mattered here was that the ratio was under control and would move downwards over time. This would be the case if Greece kept its annual budget running at or close to balance.

There was clearly uncertainty at the time whether Greece had really done enough to meet the convergence requirements and put its public finances onto a sustainable footing. The Council could (and probably should) have decided that Greece needed to demonstrate that it could maintain convergence and continue to meet the entry requirements over a longer time period. Had Greece's position really changed that dramatically since the first wave of member countries were granted entry in January 1999, when Greece failed to meet the economic tests of low inflation and government debt and deficits? One can only assume that getting Greece into the eurozone was a political imperative, even if at the time there were concerns about the reliability of the data used to justify its entry. Many investors had grave concerns surrounding the decision to allow Greece to join the euro, feeling this gave out a message that other, weaker economies might be allowed into the eurozone even if they did not fully comply with the membership conditions. But the politicians wanted Greece in – and, remember, this decision was not Greece's alone to take; existing eurozone members were also complicit.

On 1 January 2002, the biggest cash changeover in history took place. It was a challenge of unprecedented dimensions that involved the banking sector, cash-in-transit companies, retailers, the cash-operated machine industry and the general public. Around €144bn was provided early by the national central banks to commercial banks (frontloading) and by these banks to retailers (sub-frontloading) to avoid bottlenecks in the supply chain. This meant that euro cash was widely available in all sectors in the first days of 2002. By 3 January 2002, 96% of all ATMs in the euro area were dispensing euro banknotes. And just one week after the introduction, more than half of all cash transactions were being conducted in euros.

The cash changeover was completed within two months. National banknotes and coins ceased to be legal tender by the end of February 2002 in all member states and earlier in some. By that time, more than six billion national banknotes and close to thirty billion national coins had been withdrawn, and for over 300 million citizens in twelve countries the euro had finally arrived.

Everybody thought that everything was going well across Europe. The concern had been that the introduction of euro notes and coins in 2002 would (and did) lead to a huge rise in price levels, not just in Greece but across all member countries. The next concern was wage levels, especially in the less prosperous European states as they moved towards the European average – productivity, however, did not follow.

The financial markets took the euro and European Monetary Union at face value as interest rates on sovereign debts for euro members converged to a single rate. This created many problems. The markets assumed that Greek debt was as reliable as German debt, which it wasn't. And that the Germans and the eurozone collectively would stand behind the debts of its members. This was quite an assumption, one perhaps encouraged by the 'watering down' of the Stability and Growth Pact in 2005 on the part of France and Germany as soon as it looked like they would be subject to sanctions for running excessive budget deficits.

The weakness of the Stability and Growth Pact in enforcing fiscal discipline was matched by a weakness on the part of the eurozone and the European institutions to provide the 'weaker' members of the eurozone with enough help with investment and the right technical assistance to reform and modernise their economies. The pact failed to deliver growth or stability!

Meanwhile the euro had some rather predictable effects, with Spain and Ireland suffering asset bubbles because interest rates were simply too low for them.

There was no convergence in terms of productivity and unit wage costs. Figure 5.4 presents Eurostat data for labour productivity, measured by output per hour worked. It shows that, over the period from 2000 to 2010, relative productivity hardly changed. There was a slight improvement in Spain's productivity relative to Germany whereas Italy suffered a big loss of productivity relative to the European average.

FIGURE 5.4: LABOUR PRODUCTIVITY IN GERMANY AND THE PERIPHERY

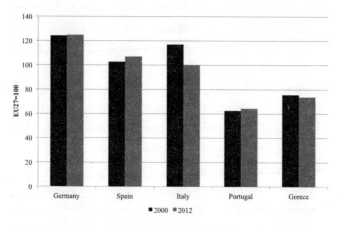

Source: Eurostat. Measure of productivity is labour productivity per hour worked.

Germany decided to become more competitive, reduced its unit labour costs and thus benefited from huge intra-Union increases in trade because of the disappearance of the balance of payments constraint.

With Greece's inflation rate on entry to the eurozone above the average, and possibly having been kept artificially low to secure entry, it is no surprise that the interest rate set for the eurozone was too low for Greece. The effect was that people and companies overborrowed and, with no ability to devalue its currency, Greek exports suffered. But Greece's debt problem is public, not private, and while cheap money can raise private borrowing, public borrowing is determined by the appetite that markets have to lend to a sovereign country. And there the problem was not membership of the euro but the presumption that this membership entitled Greece (and others) to interest rates that were almost identical to Germany's.

Greece did not use the enhanced competitive pressures of euro membership – a tighter and more credible anti-inflationary policy and the end of currency devaluation – as the impetus for the reforms it needed to preserve its competitiveness. Most of the additional spending facilitated by low interest rates went on consumption, imports and increasing the cost – though not the efficiency – of the public sector. Serious productive investments only happened because of the Olympics.

The deeper-rooted problems in its economic and political system were not addressed. Identifying the 'closed circuit' or corporatist system of politicians, bankers, the media and a small number of business operators, Louka Katseli has argued that stock market growth has been confined to just over a hundred larger firms. The money is being recycled, in the form of loans and stock options, followed by state guarantees at times of difficulty to those firms for the benefit of their owners and, of course, the banks. For Greece to have been able to benefit as it should have done from euro membership, this institutional stranglehold should have been dealt with early on, but it wasn't. Bank regulation was weak and there was little transparency. And the role of the central bank and the commercial banks has hardly been scrutinised at all.

We now see that there are similar problems in other countries, as the banking crisis in Spain has demonstrated. A closer, more integrated, better-regulated and supervised banking system across Europe would have made a huge difference. But the ability of the EU institutions to exercise that role was non-existent and whole nations have failed as a result. What we have seen in terms of the various bail-out packages so far is that most of the money still goes to rescue the banking system rather than directly help the countries in difficulty. It may be argued that of course this is crucial in ensuring that economies do not collapse when a credit crunch develops, but the eco-system in the country that has led to these problems in the first place needs to be shaken up and changed, according to Professor Katseli, so the countries can then become truly open to competition and flourish. We could be heading in this direction. The IMF conditions for the Spanish banking rescue include a tight scrutiny and monitoring of banks' activities; the memorandum of understanding between the troika and Spain calls for 'a further strengthening of the independence of the Banco de España' and demands that 'supervisory procedures of Banco de España will be further enhanced'. Spain was also condemned for the misselling of subordinated bank securities, which customers bought believing that they were similar to bank deposits and therefore safe. Greater transparency in the future was called for and Spanish accounting principles were questioned. These are moves in the right direction but rather late in the day and the costs will be significant.

So it is clear that the institutions as they existed and their role as supervisors of banking activities across Europe (and Ireland is also a case in point) were wholly inadequate to ensure that financial markets (which are the backbone of the economy) were functioning properly and transparently, and to the benefit of the economy as a whole. Professor Katseli believes that the IMF team in Greece has only scratched the surface and there is a huge amount that still needs to be done. In fact, their interventions and the bail-outs are if anything perpetuating this problem by financing the banks but not really dealing with the underlying structural problem of interlocked vested interests. Shockingly, after the bank loan crisis, it has become apparent that non-performing loans have continued to be given state guarantees signed by the Finance Minister, which have kept banks and businesses going, costing the taxpayer dear. This shows the way in which the system works, namely very close links between politicians, banks and big companies. It is also now emerging that many of these funds may well have been disappearing into offshore bank accounts.

IF A PICTURE PAINTS A THOUSAND WORDS...
Many of the woes of Greece, and the eurozone as a whole, can be summarised in Figure 5.5.

FIGURE 5.5: INTEREST RATE ON TEN-YEAR GOVERNMENT BONDS

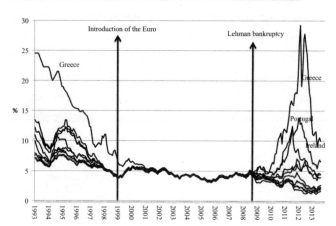

Source: European Central Bank data. Figure modelled on version from American Enterprise Institute.

The figure presents ECB data on ten-year bond yields for each of the founding members of the eurozone (with the exception of Luxembourg), the ten-year yield being seen as a benchmark figure for sovereign debt, which of course can vary in length of repayment period. Differences in yields between countries reflect differences in the markets' views on the likelihood of default.

During the 1990s we see large differences in yields between countries (i.e. the different lines are far apart) but, in the run-up to monetary union, these differences narrow. We might have expected to see this as the Maastricht entry criteria placed a strong emphasis on low inflation, tightly managed public finances and manageable levels of public debt. So countries aiming to be in the euro at the start, if they were not already in that position, had to change their policies to 'make it to Maastricht' – or at least be credibly moving in the right direction.

Even so, the almost immediate convergence of yield rates when the euro comes into being as a non-cash currency is striking. The markets clearly believed that the eurozone as a whole would stand behind the debts of any of its members in an emergency, even if there was a 'no-bail-out' clause in the Treaty. And so, when it too joined the euro slightly after the original eleven, the yield on Greek bonds fell to the same rate as that for Germany and the other eurozone members.

This pattern lasted right until 2008 and the financial crisis. Data for the five countries that joined the eurozone after notes and coins were introduced – Slovenia, Slovakia, Malta, Cyprus and Estonia – are not shown here because they would complicate the chart even further. However, much the same happened there too (with the exception of Estonia, which joined after 2008 and without significant government debt). Yields for these countries also rapidly fell to the eurozone average.

Then along came the collapse of Lehman Brothers and the financial crisis. The markets abruptly decided they could no longer safely assume that all eurozone sovereign debt was as safe as Germany's and hence they had to price each country realistically on its own merits – the 'no-bail-out' clause might after all be enforced. It is then that we see yields start to diverge and to such a high rate for Greece, Ireland and

Portugal that in effect they were shut out of international markets and forced to seek bail-outs.

NO MEETING OF MINDS

The problem with Greece since the first bail-out became necessary in May 2010 following its effective exclusion from the international money markets is that there has been little or no coming together of minds – both within Greece and certainly between Greece and its creditors, and those in whose hands its fate now lies.

Politicians in Greece continue to blame their rivals. In a recent paper published by the London School of Economics's Hellenic Observatory, George Alogoskoufis, Finance Minister under New Democracy from 2004 to 2008, argues that it was the Andreas Papandreou government of the 1980s and its lavish spending programmes that sent Greece's public debt skywards and that New Democracy in the years following euro membership had kept the public finances under control. Similarly, he argues that it was Pasok's handling of the budget deficit – in particular, disclosure of the 'real' size of it – shortly after it regained power in 2009 that spooked the markets and set in train the crisis of confidence that led to the first bail-out. Pasok ministers in riposte point out that the inflation of the Greek deficit – and the misleading estimates of its size – happened on New Democracy's watch.

Perhaps we should not be too surprised by this blame game – it is the meat and drink of politics. The political parties in the UK also phrase their rhetoric in much the same way. The coalition government says today's problems were caused by the overspending of its Labour predecessor while for senior Labour politicians it is the current government that has made matters worse by sticking to its austerity programme even when the current weakness of the economy is crying out for some easing of the fiscal targets. Nevertheless, differences about the past make it more difficult to reach the necessary consensus for the way forward. Having said that, every single Greek politician I have spoken to would accept they have not done enough over the years to reform the political system and the public sector and increase its effectiveness – and that pressing ahead with reform must be a priority for the future.

More significant – and arguably less understood – is that there has been a lack of transparency and thus a lack of trust pervading the negotiations over the two bail-outs and, in addition, the monitoring of their implementation. Put very simply, the Greeks feel that other Europeans, in particular the Germans, and the troika do not understand the sheer difficulty that Greece is in, do not see that their problems are only partly self-inflicted, and do not comprehend just how painful and difficult it has been and will be for Greece to deliver what is expected of it. Those on the other side of the table see a Greek government that cannot be trusted. Even if it is telling the truth (not guaranteed), it cannot be relied on to stick to its word or have the willingness – sometimes even the ability – to deliver on its promises.

Greece has been what ex-Prime Minister Papandreou calls 'an icebreaker', clearing a path that others would end up following. For a year or so after the first bailout, the Greeks had been the 'poster boy', performing well until spring 2011. The deficit had been reduced in a single year (2009/10) by over 5% of GDP, and the government had made big changes to pension systems and healthcare, exports had grown by 30% to 40%, and local government had been consolidated from fifty-seven regions to thirteen. Yet in spring 2011, the IMF declared that the markets were no longer going to fund Greece. Why?

The reason was a change of tone and policy by the European leaders. Peer Steinbrück, who had been the German Finance Minister until 2009, had calmed the markets by making it clear in various statements that Germany would be supporting Greece. The G20 meeting in Deauville in May 2011 changed everything, with the German Chancellor, Angela Merkel, and the then French President, Nicolas Sarkozy, making it clear that if the private sector was to invest in a higher-risk country, and that country was to default, then the private sector would have to take on the burden itself. Their reason for doing this was, of course, to reduce the cost to the taxpayer. George Papandreou, however, told them it would have an impact on the costs faced by those borrowing because the private sector, not surprisingly, would increase the risk premium for any higher-risk country. In Papandreou's view the attempt by 'Merkozy' to claim the private sector alone should bear the risk of the eurozone's poor design was the tipping point when Greece started to slide away from any stabilisation of its perilous debt problem. It was the turning point for Greece, leading to a sharp increase in sovereign yields and a reduction in its ability to borrow. Confidence plummeted and the recession deepened, with the disastrous consequences that we are seeing now.

The subsequent discussions leading to the second bail-out were therefore painful. The political situation in Greece was difficult for the government. New Democracy, in opposition at the time, was not cooperating with Pasok during the negotiations. There seemed to be no sense of national interest, only party political interest. New Democracy clearly believed that cooperation would do them no good in terms of their chances in a forthcoming election. With a very slender majority it was difficult for Papandreou to get any agreement or push too hard. Papandreou only had a majority of two or three votes. A decision to vote against him by just a few Pasok MPs or by ambitious senior ministers happy to see Papandreou ousted would have led to a government defeat and still further loss of EU confidence in the ability of Athens to manage the crisis. Hence Papandreou's belief that a clear-the-air referendum in which Greek voters would have risen above petty party politics and made clear their wish to stay in the euro (thus implicitly accepting difficult reform measures) was a pre-requisite for moving forward. It would also, in his view, have taken away the need for fresh elections. However, as Papandreou argues, New Democracy had powerful links with the ruling parties of both Germany and France, as Merkel and Sarkozy were prominent in the European People's Party, the pan-European federation of centre-right parties in which New Democracy and its leaders were long-standing active senior members. Thus when Merkel and Sarkozy reacted violently against Papandreou's referendum proposal they were serving the political interests of their New Democracy political comrades, whose main objective was to discredit Papandreou and Pasok and obtain fresh elections.

The negotiators of the second bail-out had to bear all of this in mind and ultimately the answer to making progress was a technocratic government. The negotiations for the second bail-out were finally agreed in late February 2012. Sony Kapoor, managing director of Re-Define, an economic and financial think tank, and visiting fellow of the London School of Economics, has argued that for a long time many key policy makers didn't understand the situation: they argued that all that needed to happen was a 'haircut' that reflected a change in the net present value (NPV) of the debts, in other words a change in the interest rate or the length of the loans but no cut in the face value of the loans. That seemed to be the position of the Germans at the eurozone crisis summit in Brussels of 21 July 2011, with no willingness at that stage to give way. It then took six months to finally reach the agreement with most of the private holders of debt, known as the private sector involvement (PSI) agreement, for a 53% 'haircut' on face value and an even bigger 'haircut' in practice due to a further reduction in the NPV as rates charged were reduced and the period over which loans were repaid was lengthened to at least fifteen years. Anything else would have been deemed insufficient and would have spooked the markets. Those hedge funds and others who decided not to participate were compensated, in terms of triggering credit default swap payments, and the Greeks made payments due to them anyway before the bailout was in fact concluded.

Was this a good outcome? Well, it certainly calmed the markets. They had been expecting some solution and a substantial haircut but were disappointed that the ECB and other sovereign holders of debt did not participate. But the process was a dreadful one. Because of the lack of meeting of minds it had taken forever to negotiate.

During that period the uncertainty and political chaos that ensued cost Prime Minister Papandreou his job. It was a calamity for Greece and potentially for the rest of Europe as the European leaders failed to see that this was not just a Greek problem but also one that would affect the rest of Europe in ways that would necessitate major change. And yet the remarkable sequence of events should have been a warning.

Papandreou had gone to Brussels in October 2011 to negotiate a new bail-out agreement. It was clear that the Greeks had plenty more to do and there were further cuts that needed implementing but he thought that the package would allow for an organised reduction of Greece's debt. There were of course 'haircut' discussions: in July the talk had been of haircuts of perhaps 20–25% for the private sector; by the autumn discussions were already around the 50% mark. On his return from the summit he encountered serious resistance and there was a lot of opposition from New Democracy, the media and of course the banking community, all strongly against the severity of the haircuts. As the banks would also need to be recapitalised that would change the power relationship between the government and the banks, another point of discontent.

Papandreou had limited options. The first option was fresh elections – the time at which everyone reveals their intentions. But the risk was that the various political parties would declare themselves in favour of staying in the euro but against the specifics of any package that would keep Greece in the single currency. Another option was a coalition with New Democracy but Antonis Samaras, their leader, keenly ambitious to become Prime Minister, had been against that idea. So Papandreou travelled to the G20 emergency summit in Cannes in early November 2011 having proposed a referendum so he would have the backing of the people. In the referendum the question would have been a simple one, designed to test whether the Greek people were prepared to accept the package of measures necessary to keep Greece in the eurozone. Papandreou arranged a meeting with Merkel and Sarkozy to explain his plans, which he believed were the only way to ensure the implementation of the package.

The thinking behind this bold move was that, in Greece, a large-scale game of poker was being played. Politicians were mindful of the likelihood of fresh elections given Pasok's thin majority and were positioning themselves accordingly. With so much internal opposition, Papandreou could not be confident that he could implement whatever package of spending cuts and structural reforms was agreed – and he certainly did not want to return to Brussels in three to six months and have to admit that he would fail. It seemed better to have a 'yes' or 'no' referendum, with his expectation that he would get a 'yes'. Papandreou felt confident on his way to Cannes in the run-up to the G20 summit; he had already discussed the possibility of a referendum with Merkel at a meeting in Berlin in September 2011 and he believed she had been sympathetic to the idea. He believed she was positive again in principle at Cannes although her initial statements after discussions with him were unhelpful. Sarkozy was far more negative; he was concerned about the impact on the summit, which he was chairing, as well as how the markets would perceive it. In the end Merkel and Sarkozy came out strongly against Papandreou's referendum proposal and he went back home with a very public flea in his ear. It was humiliating. The Greek public had no desire to leave the euro, let alone have a referendum on it.

When Papandreou returned to Greece he met a furore of criticism. The end result was his resignation and the appointment of a largely technocratic government, headed by a non-political figure, Lucas Papademos, but with some participation from the main political parties, New Democracy and Pasok. The government also had a relatively short mandate, its remit being to negotiate the second bail-out and push the necessary laws through Parliament. In contrast, Mario Monti's government in Italy was entirely technocratic and was given a longer period of time to implement reforms before elections were held in 2013, this time returning a left-right coalition under Enrico Letta. The coalition vowed to continue with the austerity policies, though the temporary withdrawal of ministers faithful to Silvio Berlusconi in September 2013 underlined the shaky nature of Italian governments.

There was also a gap in understanding Greece's priorities. Papandreou felt that the problems of Greece are primarily structural: clientelism, closed shops, lack of transparency, bureaucracy, corruption, lack of investment in growth areas with the investment only directed into protected groups, all creating bubbles and a mismanaged economy. Putting this right is where the focus of reform needed to be. European leaders originally agreed with this but, as time progressed, their views became more orthodox and their main mistake was confusing 'austerity' with 'reform'. The real problem was an uncompetitive economy, which the troika realised after a year or so and then wondered why there had not been enough action to deal with this. Papandreou claims that he had told them this. The necessary laws had been passed for reform, but the problem was how to implement these reforms. It took a long time for the EU to realise that Greece needs to be provided with a massive amount of technical and financial assistance. Eventually, in response to a request from Papandreou, Commission President José Manuel Barroso set up an EU Task Force for Greece funded by the Economic and Financial Affairs Council (ECOFIN), under the former senior Commission official Horst Reichenbach. There are today more than fifty EU officials working on these issues. It was a slow start and the Greeks originally treated them with great suspicion but even now they are slowly bringing in a team of experts to push best practice in the area of structural reform.

They are also looking at how to improve the flow and efficiency of structural funds into Greece which have tended not to be deployed even if assigned, as the Greeks were rarely able to provide the necessary percentage of matching funds, a condition which has now been partly relaxed. The lengthy procrastinations meant that over the period of the negotiations the situation in Greece deteriorated so significantly that the 'haircut' ended up being considerably larger than what was originally envisaged and considered sufficient just a few months earlier, also triggering a (technical) default. The markets' belief that political leaders could sort things out was damaged forever. Much of what we have seen since, particularly the testing of Spain and Italy, can be traced at least in part to the weaknesses in decision making seen during this episode.

Who is to blame for this weakness in decision making? It is easy to blame the Germans but I truly believe that during the whole negotiating process for both bail-outs the Greeks did themselves no favours. Instead of capitalising on the tremendous efforts they had made during the first year of the crisis to reduce the deficit from nearly 15% to just over 10%, they managed to completely irritate their interlocutors because they could not properly explain to anyone, particularly the Germans, why this progress was difficult to maintain and they were thus branded awkward and unwilling to shift. Much of this was their fault. Bureaucratic reform was forgotten during that time and political fights were raging. The politicians kept promising a lot but doing very little. An OECD report prepared in 2011 but published in early 2012 was disparaging of Greece's ability to reform. It argued that strong measures need to be implemented immediately to improve the effectiveness, accountability and integrity of the public administration so that it is 'fit for purpose'. This is a priority, perhaps even the first of the reform priorities, facing Greece. In other words, it argued that a failure to improve public governance in Greece would jeopardise the broader reforms that Greece needs to put into place to get back on a path to sustainable growth. And, in reality, one has seen that at every turn the inefficiency of the system has been a major source of concern for the troika, as has the politicians' seeming lack of desire to implement reform at the pace Greece's creditors would have liked to have seen. When outlining their key recommendations the OECD report made a number of stark statements that should send shivers down the spines of anyone negotiating with Greece – as well as the Greeks themselves. I have picked a few:

- There is no evident overall strategic vision to provide purpose and direction to the long-term future of the Greek society and economy, as well as for the short, medium and long-term measures to be implemented.
- Pervasive issues of corruption can be linked to the political and public administration culture and its opaque, entangled systems.
- The Greek government is not joined up and there is very little coordination which compromises reforms that need collective action.
- Implementation of policies and reforms is a major and debilitating weakness, due to a combination of a weak central supervision and a culture that favours regulatory production over results.
- There are crucial shortcomings in data collection and management which stand in the way of effective and evidence-based reforms.

And finally...

- The Greek administration is caught up in a complex legal framework (which) discourages initiative ... and blocks reform progress.

On that evidence would you really expect a country which you have already happily accepted into the single currency – and let it carry on getting richer without forcing upon it any major reform – to be capable in just three years of turning around centuries of bureaucratic obfuscation (of which the Greeks are masters – why else is 'byzantine' used as a shorthand term)? To be done by a civil service demoralised through wholesale salary and benefit cuts and with a continuous threat of redundancy? And with no incentive at the end of the line, except more of the same?

This inability to effect change clearly hasn't helped but increased Greece's difficulties, which have been poorly understood by the rest of Europe. It is widely believed that the main stumbling block in getting an agreement for the second bail-out was the Germans, who just didn't understand the Greek situation. A gulf developed with the Greeks unable to convey to the Germans the difficulty of achieving the fiscal reduction targets even if there had been the best will in the world and if the population had been behind them – which it obviously wasn't (hence the violent demonstrations on the streets). Yes, much could be done in the medium to long term with the right incentives, elimination of corruption and a further substantial reduction of the public sector. But that takes time and also requires a level of administrative efficiency that Greece just does not have yet, as well as the ability to point to some light at the end of the tunnel, which just was not and still is not visible.

For all its faults, Greece is a symptom rather than the cause of the eurozone crisis; the origins of the crisis lie in the flaws in the system. Essays focusing on Greece as a way to solve the euro crisis confuse cause and effect. Greece is the victim, not the cause, of the failure of the early 21st-century European economic system and the flawed euro project. The Spanish, Italian and other crises have shown that Greece is far from alone. But Greece seems now to symbolise all that is wrong with the seemingly lazy, corrupt Mediterranean countries which should never have been allowed to join as they drag the whole system down. There are so many fundamental flaws with that argument, not least the benefit that central European countries have enjoyed as a result of these periphery countries having the same (and for them overvalued) exchange rate. Even Open Europe, a right-wing UK think tank, has calculated that if Greece were to leave the euro now it would still need huge support from the IMF and others, including quite likely the UK, totalling €259bn in the short term. That does not even include what they assume will have to be extra long-term support or any estimate of the contagion costs to the rest of the eurozone, which of course could be immense.

A Greek exit and reintroduction of the drachma would be a catastrophe. So it is clearly in no country's interest that, despite such a flawed system, Greece should exit. But it remains sadly true that the Greeks need to change their spots, or at least cover them up, if they are to be taken seriously and helped from here on. As I argued earlier, this is not only in the interest of the Greeks but of the eurozone countries as a whole. A bit of understanding and help would go a long way to correct the situation.

THE SOCIAL COST OF AUSTERITY

The impact of the crisis on Greece has been devastating as democracy suffered and tempers flared. There were violent demonstrations on the streets, shops were looted, the politicians themselves started fearing for their own safety, the centre of Athens became a no-go area for a while and for a year there were five serious strikes a week. No country can survive that for any length of time without serious repercussions. The fabric of society started to fall apart at the seams.

As all countries are cutting back to achieve some form of fiscal consolidation, the focus on the human costs of the policies has only just started to surface. I heard some Germans participating in a panel at a Bloomberg event in July 2012 explain the philosophy of reform that allowed Germany to increase its competitiveness significantly in the last ten years. This was a model that combined structural change, including reform of the labour market and collective bargaining systems, with slow wage growth (falling in some industries in real terms) but combined with a certainty of welfare support that keeps the social fabric in place while changes happen. In some cases, like Spain and France, the cuts, until recently at least, had been carried out against a background of very generous pension and unemployment benefits. Indeed, countries like France and Germany pay unemployment benefits that average some 65–75% of net incomes for people who have lost their jobs. This compares with just under 50% if you are lucky, and had actually been contributing, in Greece. Spain, which announced a cut of 30% in the actual benefit paid, had, in common with France, been providing unemployment benefits for two years after someone lost their job. In Greece, it has been one year with nothing paid unless you have contributed appropriately. This means that young people who are unemployed rely on their parents or other family members or charities to support them. And of course that has severe side effects. Direct housing benefits are negligible. Most of the housing budget of the Greek government goes on construction of homes rather than supporting families that are unable to pay the rent. The result is that people are either being evicted and are on the streets with little support or, if they are lucky, the landlords keep them on at little or no rent if they still manage somehow to pay the electricity and keep the place safe! They are the lucky ones, but everyone loses in terms of purchasing power and the economy suffers.

The OECD has been involved in an exercise to review the whole benefit system in Greece, except health and pensions, which have been undergoing some reform under the first bail-out. The troika in its wisdom had also expected that the reform of the social benefits system might contribute to the improvement of the deficit by 1.5% of GDP in the three years to 2013. This is large in relation to the overall improvement needed and, if implemented without attention to the indirect consequences of any measures, could be socially explosive. True, there is quite a lot that can be done through streamlining the provision of benefits but there are too many bodies involved. Aside from the Ministry of Labour, there is no oversight of the interactions between the whole tax and benefits system with the Ministry of Finance too busy with concerns over short-term measures to cut the debt and its negotiations with the troika on the various bail-outs to develop an overall strategy of what might work best in the Greek environment. One international civil servant, who has been looking at Greece and is sympathetic to its plight, says it is a shame in a way that Greece is not a developing country. If it was, it could start from scratch and set up a system that would work. But systems, however inefficient, do exist, data are produced, however incomplete, and throwing it all out and starting again would cause huge disruption and hardship. A way, therefore, has to be found to simplify, streamline and improve the current system and achieve greater efficiency.

There have been changes, of course, and the Greek government has been trying to streamline the various social security funds that exist for different classes of contributors to make some savings. Lots of countries, including the UK, have been grappling with such issues for decades. The problems are not easy but they cannot be avoided, especially at a time of severe strain on the finances. So Greece should be looking at a number of possible avenues ahead. Should there, for example, be more effective means testing? Are there perverse incentives that affect other areas of policy with unintended consequences that can be tackled? An example is the rule that, if one has worked for four months in Greece and then been made redundant, one is entitled to seven months of unemployment benefit. So companies hire workers for four months, then fire them, the worker then signs on to the dole drawing benefit, is then rehired illegally by the firm (not paying crippling social security contributions and tax) for the next seven months, and everyone wins – except the state and the taxpayers who have to foot the bill!

The next question is, are the benefits going to the right people? One policy being looked at is family help given to people with three and more children, becoming more generous the more children you have and often staying with you and your children forever even if they have left home. If, like me, you have more than four children, the state provides you with an extra monthly payment of €98 for life! Smaller families get little support and single mothers naturally suffer, although Greece has one of the lowest numbers of single mothers in Europe. In addition, there are arguably too many different categories of benefits and there is huge abuse of the system as a result. A particular example is disability benefits, which are given to far too big a percentage of the population. There are so many different definitions of blindness that anyone, with a little help from their friendly physician, can find a category to fit in. Indeed there is a well-known tourist island where apparently some 90% of its inhabitants draw benefits as officially blind! The tourists appear not to have noticed.

But whatever is done must always be done with an eye on the impact of poverty in Greece. The present system is hardly generous, except for providing disability benefits. Means testing, badly done, could send even more people into poverty. Poverty levels in Greece were the highest of any country in the eurozone before the crisis. The usual definition is being 60% below the median income, though we must beware statistics, as given the very sharp decline in the median income, the poverty rate may in fact have fallen slightly during the recession. But visible signs of poverty have increased in Greece, whether it is the homelessness problem or families with children that rely on soup kitchens. Businesses have gone bust at a record rate and shops lie empty. The unemployment rate continues to rise and is now the second highest in Europe – see Figure 5.6. The economy is declining further and money is fleeing the country.

FIGURE 5.6: UNEMPLOYMENT RATES ACROSS THE EUROPEAN UNION, AUGUST 2013

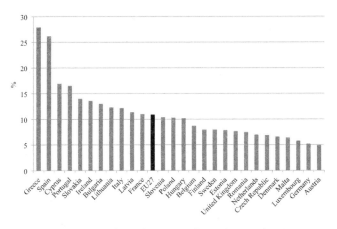

Source: Eurostat. Harmonised unemployment rates for population aged 15–74.

Concern about the impact of austerity measures is not confined to Greece. Social protests took off in Spain in the summer of 2012. Even King Juan Carlos spoke of his own concerns at the impact of the austerity measures at a Cabinet meeting on 13 July 2012, a couple of days after the measures were announced, reportedly saying, 'No one should be excluded from the outcome of the economic recovery that we want and hope for ... particularly the young and those who suffer a lack of employment and prospects for the future.'

Are there different ways to go about sorting out the structural problems of a country, without throwing people into poverty or taking away hope from the young? The latest conditions by the troika for the second Greek bail-out included a cut in the minimum

111

wage, which was already at very low levels. Greeks would in fact be pushed to near poverty levels if this were implemented. In my view, the minimum wage probably needs to be pushed up again, not only for social but also for economic reasons, in order to maintain purchasing power.

Interestingly, one of the first things that François Hollande did in France after he was elected President in May 2012 was to increase the minimum wage by 2%, not by as much as the unions wanted, but still sending an important signal. At the same time, he increased taxes on the wealthy and reinstated overtime taxes on companies with more than twenty employees, which had been cut by President Sarkozy and which had been offset in the public finances by an increase in sales tax.

That is another debate. Have the tax increases imposed by the troika on countries like Greece been the right approach? Superficially, VAT increases have the advantage of being easy to impose and administratively easy to collect, an attractive proposition in countries where tax evasion is the rule. This is based on the assumption, though, that you can force shops – either through fear of prosecution or by a change in incentives – to hand you a receipt with the VAT on it. Amazingly, in Italy and Greece, campaigns to ensure that receipts are produced by kiosks and corner shops with each purchase have been the result of customers insisting that they be handed one each time they shop. I have watched elderly ladies arguing with kiosk owners and then walking off triumphantly brandishing a receipt.

It is also arguable that in some countries, like the UK, the balance of tax had to see a shift from direct to indirect as it had gone too much the other way in previous decades. But sales tax increases, which have been very much part of IMF-inspired bail-out packages, can have a number of unintended consequences. They raise prices and therefore reduce the purchasing power of mostly people with lower incomes. They tend to lead to wage earners demanding increases to compensate, which then have the effect of raising price levels further, making a country uncompetitive. In times of hardship, when that is not possible, they tend instead to make people spend less and often defeat the purpose of the exercise by reducing domestic demand. This is exactly the situation that has been observed in Greece. Louka Katseli says that the sharp increase in excise taxes coupled with dramatic wage and pension cuts has exacerbated the recession with negative consequences on tax returns and public deficit reduction. This has been the wrong policy for the country and has contributed to the situation becoming worse rather than better after the first year of dramatically cutting the deficit. She thinks the Greeks should have used the flexibility within the bail-out to enhance net revenues by other means, most notably by fighting tax evasion, expanding the tax base, revamping social benefits, rationalising health expenditure, promoting electronic governance and introducing bold administrative reforms.

The jury is still out on that. But what is clear is that VAT increases and wage cuts should be looked at very carefully at times of weak economic growth as they can in fact lead to lower, rather than higher, tax receipts and a worsening, rather than an improvement, in the deficit.

A DISAFFECTED POPULATION

The elections on 17 June 2012 were highlighted by the largest abstention rate ever (38.7%), higher than in the inconclusive 6 May 2012 elections, and by the rise of Alexis Tsipras, the young leader of a left splinter party that went from 4.5% in 2009 to 17% in May 2012 and 27% in June 2012. It also saw the emergence of the far right in unprecedented numbers.

A strong showing by the left is not surprising in a country that has been flirting with Communism for decades, but the rise of the right is not just due to disdain for the mainstream parties – it would also appear to be a reaction to lawlessness and uncontrolled immigration. Greece is the most porous, most popular border for EU entry from the east, used by Albanians, Arabs, Asians and Africans. Whereas the geography of the land and its archipelago make it easy to enter, it is difficult to find ways to move onto other EU states. So, instead of a transit point, those who get stuck try to make a living in a country that cannot even provide for its own.

Greece is left practically unaided to defend its own and therefore Europe's borders. The country does not have the resources to prevent immigrants from coming through its porous borders or to provide for their numbers once they settle in Greece. Only a fraction of the illegal entrants get caught at the border or through ID checks once they have gained entry.

The immigration issue has been blamed for the inflation in crime statistics. According to the latest statistics, 64% of the crimes resolved were committed by foreigners as opposed to 14% committed by Greeks (it is not clear who committed the other 22%). Caution should be exercised when interpreting any Greek statistics, however. There may be all sorts of administrative biases which make it easier to tick off a crime as 'resolved' if it can be pinned on an immigrant. But this is what the statistics say and the message being spun from this is that, if Greece got rid of its illegal population, it would be a much safer, less anxious society. That's what the far right is saying and some of the public and politicians are buying the message.

Greece, Spain and Italy are not only champions of sovereign debt, they also lead the world in low birth rates. These three Mediterranean and supposedly religious nations have rates that hover around 1%. Low birth rates are also experienced in other European countries, except where immigrants constitute a significant minority. A social system that was built on a ratio of four workers for every one retiree in the baby boom days is shrinking fast to an unsustainable ratio of two to one. A much increased life expectancy of about eighty years adds to the challenge of providing the means of subsistence and social services from shrinking resources.

With high overall unemployment and with, as shown in Figure 5.7, youth unemployment exceeding 50%, the current (short-term) bail-out measures could have devastating long-term impacts, as they will change the demographics of Greece. Families are following breadwinners to other countries. Those who cannot negotiate their migration are pushing their children out, initially to foreign educational institutions, to find opportunity and to provide for their families in the future.

FIGURE 5.7: UNEMPLOYMENT RATES FOR YOUNG PEOPLE ACROSS THE EUROPEAN UNION, AUGUST 2013

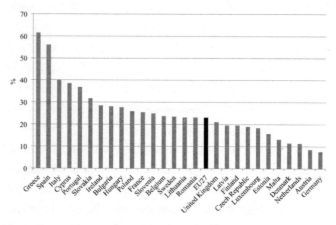

Source: Eurostat. Harmonised unemployment rates for population aged 15–24.

Greece is suffering an enormous brain drain and a population reduction that will change the social and economic profile of the nation. Some claim that, at this rate, Greece will shrink to eight million people by 2050 from eleven million today, with half of the population in retirement.

Concern still rages around the fact that, since the second bail-out, little seems to have changed but the sheer level of hardship experienced by the Greek people, accentuated by further cuts announced in August 2012. Greeks are notoriously proud people – it would be with an enormous amount of reluctance that they would be prepared to admit they were going hungry. Long after discussions end over where the fault lies, it seems that those who are perhaps least to blame are paying the highest price.

In July 2013 the EU announced an €8bn two-year programme aimed at tackling youth employment. Advocated by German Chancellor Angela Merkel (under pressure as Europe's Empress of Austerity, as she became known), the sum amounts to €850 a year for every young person not in employment, education or training. It is hardly enough and the programme seems to focus on teaching young people more languages so they can travel for interviews across Europe. But it was a welcome sign that Europe's leaders recognised that anti-growth austerity measures were having some severe consequences on Europe's population, particularly the young. Although the Commission seems to disagree with the IMF on whether the austerity measures are the right medicine or not, it is increasingly clear that Greece's economy, even with minor improvements, cannot grow in a sustainable fashion under present conditions imposed from outside. Some economists reckon that Greece's population, especially its young people, suffered worse hardship than that imposed on US citizens during the Great Depression of the 1930s. Greece needs European recovery and a return to growth. In the sixth year of the crisis, was this finally being understood?

6

THE FRANCO-GERMAN RELATIONSHIP – CENTRAL TO THE PAST, PRESENT AND FUTURE

THE BACKGROUND

From medieval to modern times France was Europe's number one nation. Occasionally France fought with England and England won. But then Europe's island nation retired to enjoy its oceanic trade and empire and France re-emerged. Paris gave Europe the Enlightenment and founded the modern republican state. Its writers, fashions and elegance made Paris the city all Europe wanted to visit. And then suddenly without warning the era of France as Europe's dominant continental power ended.

Three times in the space of seven decades Germany invaded, occupied or dismembered France. The Germans seemed able to bring France crashing down in defeat at a flick of their war machine, backed by industry and a bigger, better-educated population. 'Blood and iron,' proclaimed Chancellor Bismarck as he explained to his people how and why Germany would win. Germany always did win even if France, after heroic efforts and sacrifice and with the help of the 'Anglo-Saxons' (the all-purpose dismissive phrase the French use for the Americans and the British), managed in 1918 and 1945 to be part of a victorious coalition over Germany.

So after three national humiliations at the hands of Germany in less than a century the French decided after 1945 that a new tactic was needed. Instead of a Maginot line and a reliance on military power and the occupation of Germany by the US, Russia, Britain and France, why not begin the intertwining of the two nations so that, as between the United States and Canada, conflict became unthinkable? By the middle of the twentieth century, the American and Canadian dollar became closely linked, and the American and Canadian industrial base became a common one as automobile, steel and other concerns treated the whole of North America as a common economic zone.

After 1945, Germany and France made a dramatic decision to surrender their formal national sovereignty over the steel and coal industries. Today these heavy industries remain important but are mainly seen as relics of the past. To remove steel and coal from national politics was the main object of the first European Treaty. Unsurprisingly, the European Treaty was about politics, not economics. Increased trade was a desirable outcome but the main purpose remained Franco-German relations. Trade unions were given a strong role, in line with the socially responsible capitalism advanced by the Christian Democratic Union in north and west Germany and the Christian Social Union in Franconia (part of Bavaria).

THE EUROPEAN UNION

Very little has changed even today. The history of the European Economic Community (EEC), now the European Union, has been the history of relations between France and Germany. In exchange for opening markets fully to quality German goods, France insisted upon a common system of agricultural subsidies, which benefited the efficient, profitable agro-industries of France. France was a net beneficiary of European transfer payments until the late 1990s. Germany left to France the decision to allow or deny EEC membership to the United Kingdom and acceded to France's demand for an early entry into the European Community for Greece in 1981 instead of waiting until the foundations were better laid as they were for Portugal and Spain.

In 1963, the Élysée Treaty was signed between President de Gaulle and Chancellor Adenauer. It sealed Franco-German cooperation as the cornerstone of both nations' relationship with each other and the rest of Europe. At each successive stage of European construction, France and Germany were either the leaders or had to come to agreement over what steps to take. What was always clear was that the free movement of goods and capital required political agreement of a high order. Although both countries grew strongly in terms of GDP per capita in the first period of European unity, they did so on very different terms. France remained largely state controlled. The Fourth Republic (1946–58) set in hand plans to encourage French industry, innovation and dispersal of new businesses. Under De Gaulle's Fifth Republic (1958–present) France remained largely centralised with the state owning major industries. The graduates of the École Nationale d'Administration (ENA) were an élite group of highly educated men and women who ran France's industries and state and regional administrations, and even became Presidents and Prime Ministers, including Valéry Giscard d'Estaing and François Hollande. If Louis XIV famously said '*L'état, c'est moi*', of the Énarques (ENA graduates) it was said '*L'état, c'est nous*'. They put together projects like Airbus Industrie and, working with the Coal and Steel Community, gently reduced the importance of the steel and coal sectors in France without the social strife associated with the conflict generated by Margaret Thatcher and Arthur Scargill in the 1980s.

France was not completely free of conflict, however, as the events of May 1968 showed. A pro-Soviet Communist trade union called the CGT (Confédération Générale du Travail or the General Confederation of Labour) was locked in permanent political struggle for influence with its labour movement rivals, the reformist CFDT (Confédération Française Démocratique du Travail or the French Democratic Confederation of Labour) and the pro-American and occasionally

Trotskyist FO (Force Ouvrière or the General Confederation of Labour). Indeed, until the mid-1980s, a powerful French Communist party which proclaimed its anti-capitalist, anti-European and anti-globalisation ideology commanded up to a quarter of French votes and was an important force in intellectual circles with the ability to mobilise strikes and street demonstrations. In 1981, soon after the arrival of Margaret Thatcher and Ronald Reagan announced a new era of economic thinking based on reducing the state presence, attacking social partnership and increasing the share of national income going to rentier (share-owning) income and a reduction of the share of national income going to wage and salary earners, the new President of France, the socialist François Mitterrand, announced a massive programme of nationalisations, as well as state-decreed increases in the minimum wage and a reduction in working time.

In Germany, by contrast, the opposite political economy took shape. There was no overall national economic control. The Bundesbank, in contrast to the Banque de France, was independent in terms of inter-est-rate setting. Power was decentralised to regional governments (*Länder*). Unlike the all-powerful President of France, the government of Germany was always a messy coalition with its compro-mises and trade-offs. The national or, as Germans called it, the 'federal' government in Bonn and then in Berlin could decide relatively little. Enterprises were privately owned, with some limited regional stake-holding in firms such as Volkswagen. Unlike France's powerful defence industry with its captive market at the Ministry of Defence and ministers acting as sales agents for export orders, Germany's defence capability was limited. Germany had to pay its way by producing products that would hold their own against any in the world and do so in market competition with other German firms as well as companies from outside Germany.

The organisation of firms was completely different. German trade unions opposed a minimum wage and rarely went on strike, and then only after obtaining more than 75% of support in a secret ballot vote – a rule inscribed in union constitutions, not dictated by law as in Britain. The boards of German companies were split between a supervisory board, on which representatives of unions and the firm's employees sat, and a management board. Again, this produced compromise and agreement by dialogue rather than diktat. Companies operated within a devolved regional structure and no single German city came to dominate economic decision making in the manner of Paris or London. German unions negotiated, first, weekends off for workers in the 1950s, then four-, six- and seven-week holidays and, finally, at the end of the 1980s, the high point for the German economic model before the fall of the Berlin Wall, a 35-hour week for all industrial workers. Local works councils could also cut more flexible deals. It is a paradox of the German model that it flouted most of the rules of what is prescribed elsewhere – i.e. longer hours, reduced labour union presence and the ability to fire workers easily – which are all seen as necessary to restore economic confidence in today's Europe! In exchange for this social power and partnership the trade unions have always accepted the need to maintain German companies' competitiveness. Hence, they accepted the plans put forward by Gerhard Schröder for the recapitalisation of German industry at the end of 1990s.

INTEGRATION OF WEST AND EAST GERMANY

In 1990, Germany seemed to have discovered the philosopher's stone of strong economic performance, a massive balance of trade surplus driven by its exports, plus social investment and a move towards the green economy culminating in a disengagement with nuclear power. The abrupt end of Communism, however, brought Germany the sudden challenge of integrating the backward Third-World economy of the German Democratic Republic into the modern advanced market economy of West Germany. From one day almost to the next, sixteen million new Germans were added to the population with all the rights of the existing sixty-three million citizens of the Federal Republic. Nowhere had such a task been undertaken in recent world history. No other west European democracy had to take full responsibility for the citizens of an economy based on completely different assumptions. The impact on Germany was dramatic. Between 1992 and 1998, 160 billion Deutschmarks (DM) were spent on infrastructure in East Germany. West German growth, which recorded a 5.7% increase in 1990 and 4.7% in 1991, slumped to 2.6% in 1993 and remained low for a long period.

Today's German performance is of course much stronger than most of its EU partners and certainly far better than the troubled southern eurozone economies, but it is a pale shadow of the mighty economic machine that grew and grew until Communism imploded and the Berlin Wall came down. Germans were faced with a 5.5% solidarity tax on all income to pay for unification and there is considerable, if unspoken, resentment in Germany that the rest of Europe contributed far less, in fact nothing at all, to the raising of the living standards of those who had lived under Communism up to 1989.

By the end of the 1990s, it was clear that for Germany to win back the competitiveness it had enjoyed a decade previously a new injection of capital was needed. Capital was obtained by holding down workers' wages, with the agreement of unions, for half a decade. At the same time, the Hartz reforms (so called after their main architect, Peter Hartz, the Personnel Director of Volkswagen, who was close to Chancellor Gerhard Schröder) also introduced cheaper forms of labour contracts in a bid to keep German companies operating in Germany instead of off-shoring to Asia or other cheap labour markets. Unlike French denunciation of *délocalisation* (relocating production to another country) Berlin worked with employers' organisations to encourage German firms to set up subsidiaries in Poland, Hungary, Slovakia and the Czech Republic as the new eastern European states became part of the globalised market economy.

OPPOSITES ATTRACT

Even today, the organisation of politics, economics, labour markets and ways of seeing and doing business in France and Germany remain fundamentally different. Six decades of common membership in European supranational bodies has not seen a convergence between the two countries, which remain more French and more German than ever. Few French leaders speak German (the present Prime Minister, Jean-Marc Ayrault, a former German teacher, is a notable exception) and German Chancellors have rarely spoken French. If they have one, their common language is English. Despite the wide differences either side of the Rhine, the past, present and future of the European Union depends on France and Germany. From time to time, a British Prime Minister is admitted to this Franco-German partnership – notably Margaret Thatcher, when she was encouraged to support the Single European Act, the appointment of Jacques Delors as Commission President and the massive increase in the European Community budget in the mid-1980s. Tony Blair also briefly sought to make the duo a trio, alongside the socialist French Prime Minister, Lionel Jospin, and German Social Democrat Chancellor Gerhard Schröder.

Other countries matter, to be sure. Neither France nor Germany can impose their will either alone or even jointly unless they find majority support from other EU partners. Yet the key moments of European integration – or lack thereof – arise from the Franco-German relationship. Germany, for example, had to accept de Gaulle's insistence on the primacy of national will and the right of countries to veto developments they did not want to see happen. In the late 1970s, Helmut Schmidt and Valéry Giscard d'Estaing, joined to discuss (in English) how to create a common European monetary system. The French franc had undergone devaluations both formally – in 1969 – and informally – under the floating exchange rate systems that followed the end of the Bretton Woods system of managed exchange rates.

Both Schmidt and Giscard d'Estaing were economists and believed that, without exchange rate stability between the two countries, it would be difficult to sustain the common market. The French political left constantly called for devaluation, arguing that imports into France would slow down and exports would get a boost if the franc became weaker. Yet the opposite happened. Germany, with its strong DM, boosted exports and France, with its devalued franc, found all imports far more expensive and experienced no particular boost in exports. French companies needing to invest and do business overseas found the weak franc a hindrance not a help. The last two major devaluations of the French franc took place in 1983 and 1986 within the framework of the Exchange Rate Mechanism (ERM). The French franc was devalued by 8% and 6% respectively against the DM. But, as in the past, this devaluation brought little relief to the French economy, which was not able to produce world-beating products.

For President François Mitterrand, this enforced devaluation was both a humiliation of his claims to be leader of a powerful nation and a judgement on the first two years of his presidency. So, once again the Franco-German relationship played its part. In 1984, France and Germany decided to lock their currencies as a prelude to the Single European Act and the widening and deepening of the single market. From that period on to the launch of the euro, France and Germany (together with the Benelux nations and Denmark, which pegged its crown to the DM) had a de facto single currency. Decisions on interest rates were taken by the independent central banks but the level of coordination was such that policy makers and businesses started operating on the principle that there would be no variations in exchange rate values. The ERM system did allow for small fluctuations but French, German and Benelux business leaders and exporters woke up to find that the French franc and DM had stopped varying in their relative values. A new era of exchange rate stability, some fifteen years before the formal introduction of the euro, got underway. This contrasted to the yo-yoing of the British pound which could move from being worth little more than eight French francs to nearly thirteen francs in the space of twelve months – although, when Chancellor Nigel Lawson attempted to stabilise the British exchange rate by shadowing the DM in the late 1980s, the (indirect) consequences included imported inflation as well as him losing his job!

THE MOVE TOWARDS THE EURO

France and Germany had taken the decisive step towards laying the foundations of the single currency. The long rules of François Mitterrand (1981–95) and Helmut Kohl (1982–98), combined with Jacques Delors (1985–95) at the helm of the EU Commission, provided a Franco-German axis that dominated European affairs. Britain fell by the wayside as an EU player as John Major took over from Margaret Thatcher. Britain's economy had received a major boost from economic reforms in the 1980s but performance remained erratic and the pound sterling joined the ERM in October 1990 at a flatteringly high level. Italy opted for eccentric leaders like Bettino Craxi and Silvio Berlusconi and, although strong in defending its interests, was content to bow to the Franco-German hegemony.

The reunification of Germany saw France faced with a country that was no longer of roughly the same size as itself and with few ambitions to be a geo-political player other than maintaining open markets for its exports. Between 1950 and 1990, France and Germany had different but mutually compatible interests in Europe. After the fall of the Berlin Wall,

Paris saw its old German fears arising again. Germany was no longer the eastern outpost of a western Euro-Atlantic democratic liberal market world where France had global status as a nuclear power and a permanent member of the UN Security Council. Germany was back as the biggest nation in a Europe which now had to deal with Poland and other former Soviet bloc countries which were asserting their right to be treated as European democracies and which were shedding statist economics in favour of the prevailing liberal economic models.

LEAVING HISTORY IN THE PAST

For Paris the question was how France and Germany would form a relationship so that old rivalries and disputes would never reoccur. For the ruling German generation, born during or just after the Second World War, there was also a need to keep old German demons firmly locked away. Even so, the German constitution was changed to allow German soldiers to take part in operations outside German soil and Germany launched an unsuccessful campaign to get a seat as a permanent member of the UN Security Council. For the first time since 1950, Germany sided with France in 2003 against the United States when President Chirac and Chancellor Schröder united to oppose the invasion of Iraq.

But this political cooperation needed to be cemented into a new European design which was based on the economics of the single currency and the politics of the European Constitutional Treaty, drawn up by a convention presided over by the former French President, Valéry Giscard d'Estaing. French voters narrowly scuppered the Constitutional Treaty in a referendum in 2005 but the succeeding Lisbon Treaty was largely shaped by French officials in Brussels with the quiet backing of Berlin. Already, Laurent Fabius, today France's socialist Foreign Minister, had called for Germany and France to send a single representative to the IMF. Pierre Moscovici, now Economy, Finance and Industry Minister, had called for a single President for Europe. So the process of seeking to submerge the unqualified national identity of Germany into a shared currency and European governance with France continued as a high priority for both countries as the twenty-first century went through its first decade.

THE BANKING CRISIS

When the banking crisis of 2008 struck, the two countries were in entirely different situations. Germany had made some tough economic reforms, which cost Gerhard Schröder his chancellorship, with Social Democratic voters fed up with years of wage austerity voting him out in 2005. Angela Merkel, first in coalition with the Social Democrats and then after 2009 with the Liberal Free Democrats, had a much stronger economic base than the new French President after 2007, Nicolas Sarkozy. Sarkozy was flamboyant and excitable and a superb political animal. Yet he was all tactics and little strategy and lost the confidence of French citizens by his zigzagging policies. He was unable to read the economic crisis that broke after 2008. His own policies had been based on continuing to borrow to pay for France's expensive welfare state and generous pension systems, which his predecessors had initiated after de Gaulle left power nearly four decades earlier. As long as there was some growth in the French economy, the debt could be managed. Sarkozy had promised a breakthrough to a new economics in France but was unwilling to reduce state expenditure or dismantle many of the internal cartels that prevented a more liberal energetic economy from growing.

Without a European strategy of his own, Sarkozy decided to bind himself closely to Angela Merkel, acting as an echo-chamber for her views on Europe, giving rise to the term 'Merkozy'. As the crisis quickly became a question of payment transfers to help keep first Greece, then Ireland and Portugal, and now Spain and Italy, within the single currency, France was unable to move forward. Its own debt and deficit position and status as defined by ratings agencies left the country as the very junior partner to Germany. Sarkozy's more liberal inclinations had not been able to overcome French statist traditions and he had no vision on how to get out of the crisis other than applying austerity measures. Sarkozy saw France reduced to the status of a bystander as key decisions on the European crisis were taken by Germany.

But on one point France did not waver. The euro

was now central to French existence and identity. So too was the wider European community of nations. In the presidential election of May 2012, Nicolas Sarkozy sought to portray himself as the defender of French frontiers against all comers. He also railed against foreign workers coming in from other EU member states. Further on the right, Marine Le Pen, leader of the anti-European xenophobic *Front National* party, also denounced Europe and called for a return of the French franc. Her father, Jean-Marie Le Pen, had invented the term *fédéraste* (an 'abhorrent' attachment to European federalism). On the left, Jean-Luc Mélenchon also denounced the European Union as a capitalist, liberal, free-market conspiracy intent on crippling France. The only major candidate who calmly asserted the centrality of the European Union to France's future was François Hollande. He won the election decisively, beating the various shades of more hostile politics to Europe. His victory was confirmed with a handsome majority in the French National Assembly election in June 2012 that followed the presidential contest. Hollande's administration is full of pro-European ministers.

He himself sought a different relationship from Sarkozy with Angela Merkel, insisting on growth measures that should parallel the necessary debt and deficit reduction policies, including those in France. But while Hollande can talk growth, only Merkel has the money, thanks to the austerity years of Gerhard Schröder, to help bankroll the cries of help from the overextended banking systems facing near ruin in southern European economies. French and German banks are completely mixed up in southern Europe. Many of the loans that Greece cannot now repay were provided by German and French banks to buy German or French capital goods and arms, or to hire expertise for motorway or airport construction around the time of the 2004 Athens Olympics.

French and German banks, especially the latter's small regional *Landesbanken*, are also badly exposed and neither Berlin nor Paris have real control or even sufficient knowledge of the financial instruments and dodgy lending their own banks have got up to in the last twenty-five years of deregulated banking and financial services. As Europeans have fought for Germany to mutualise all debts and place its considerable reserves for the use of politicians in Greece, Spain or even Italy, where Silvio Berlusconi is threatening a comeback, few have bothered to acknowledge the first rule of politics: to hold power you have to win elections and to keep power you have to win re-election. Germany is the most intensely electoral nation in Europe. Federal elections take place every four years but rolling waves of regional government elections provide a constant electoral check on the authority of the federal Chancellor as the devolved system of power in Germany hands many competences to regional government.

So Mrs Merkel, rather like a US President who has to coax Congress and the Supreme Court to accept his policies, has far less political power and authority than a French President or a British Prime Minister with working majorities in their parliaments. Mrs Merkel exists in the tension of a permanent cohabitation with other political forces who control the Bundesrat (the upper house of the German Parliament). The press in Germany, which rants against a single German cent keeping reckless southern Europeans going, is also a powerful factor limiting her freedom of action.

Germany has a sensationalist tabloid press and some very self-important editors and commentators. They have enjoyed portraying Greece as lazy, corrupt and governed by shameless politicians who buy votes by spending money on public sector wages and pensions that Greece has simply not earned. The racist stereotyping by the German media of workshy, grubby, greedy Greeks is vicious, inaccurate and unfair given that Germans put in some of the shortest work hours in Europe. It is, of course, crazy to assume that the eurozone countries in crisis are full of lazy people and those that are not are bursting at the seams with hardworking individuals. Martin Wolf of the *Financial Times* says:[†] 'If one went by the hours worked on average by each worker, one would conclude that the fewer hours people work, the less crisis-prone will be the country,' and he warns: 'Beware idle moralism. It is an intellectual trap.' His article places Germany at the lower end of working hours during 2011 along

---

† Martin Wolf, 'Fallacies about work and the crisis', FT.com, 24 July 2012.

with France, and Ireland, Portugal and Greece among those with the highest average hours (mainly because these countries have relatively high proportions of self-employed, who work the longest hours).†

Greeks gave as good as they got. Mrs Merkel was depicted with a Hitler moustache, and Nazi swastikas or 'Germanophobe' references surfaced in Greek political discourse as the Greek aspect of the crisis unfolded. Paradoxically, the Greeks were much stronger in support of staying in the euro than the Germans were.

WHERE IS THE FRANCO-GERMAN RELATIONSHIP NOW?

Mrs Merkel, a deeply serious woman, does not share the crudities of her tabloid press but she did need to get re-elected in September 2013. No politician can ignore public hostility on European questions or the sense that Germans have that their own economy and banking system may not be as permanently robust as it has seemed since her arrival in power. German growth is weak. In the four years of the crisis to the first quarter of 2012, the German economy grew by 1%. This is better than the UK or the eurozone average but is hardly remarkable. But Germany also knows that its export markets depend on Europe. In 2011 Germany exported ten times as much to the rest of Europe as it did to China, with the eurozone taking 40% of made-in-Germany goods and services.

---

† Conference Board Database.

Exports to the rest of the EU account for a quarter of Germany's GDP.

Thus a disintegration of the euro into national currencies with a propensity to devalue would be disastrous for the German economy. German industrial wages have been increasing by over 4% in 2012 and public sector wages by nearly 6% so Germany is stepping up to the challenge of increasing national domestic demand. But Germany's call for the rest of Europe to adopt the German model of strong exporting companies begs the question: If Germany wants to base its economy on exports then who will import German goods? And if other European countries emulate Germany then who will buy all their exported goods? The EU as a whole still runs a balance of trade surplus but, within Europe, the very basis of Germany's economic success is the sale of German goods to other EU member states. If Greece or Spain stopped driving Mercedes and BMWs and opted for cheaper Korean models or bought more cars made in Britain by Japanese- or Indian-owned firms, would that help Germany?

CONTROL OF THE BANKS

In a sense, Germany and France may be approaching the point that both nations got to after 1945, when it was agreed to forgo national sovereignty over what were seen as supremely strategic economic sectors – the coal industry that produced energy and the steel industry that produced the material to rebuild both nations – not forgetting that joint control over these industries would make any attempt to engage in covert rearmament much more difficult. Britain refused to join, arguing that national sovereignty could not let go of control of coal and steel. Today, are the banks what coal and steel were sixty-five years ago? Is a community or union of banks what Europe needs so as to weed out the inefficient, corrupt or badly run ones with a writing off of their bad debts? It is not clear that France and Germany are ready to move in that direction. François Hollande, following Jacques Delors, who launched the idea of Eurobonds two years ago, calls for a greater Europeanisation or mutualisation of debt. Germany hints at willingness in exchange for France (and other eurozone nations) agreeing to a greater degree of supranational authority over both banking operations and how national budgets are constructed so that debt and deficits are not allowed to run out of control. To an extent, a properly managed national economy should have nothing to fear from external supervision of its practices. The Marshall Plan, after all, was based on planners from the US sitting in ministries overseeing its implementation. The housing bubbles that caused such damage in Spain and Ireland would have been stopped by rules from elsewhere in Europe, such as demanding that some down payment is made for loans to buy homes. The German practice of placing employees and unions on the boards of major companies, including banks, may stop some of the excessively self-indulgent pay deals which are disconnected from company performance.

139

Yet in 2012 the CEO of Volkswagen was allowed a €16m bonus authorised by the board, on which union workers and regional politicians were represented.

But if France wants mutualisation of German debt, will Paris accept loss of control over its banks? Will Germany want external authority over its hundreds of small regional banks, which offer seats on boards to local political bosses and cut cosy corporate deals with their *Mittelstand* clients? And how does this work within the framework of domestic politics? Or with the difficulties President Hollande faces as key French companies like Peugeot announce thousands of redundancies and factory closures? Will the old sirens of national economic control resurface? If the eurozone shrinks, will those countries forced out be tempted to turn their backs on the entire European project of economic integration, based on opening borders to the competition of outside companies and products?

THE WAY AHEAD

The answer to these questions will come from two capitals – Paris and Berlin. Other nations are important but there have only ever been two central players at the heart of the construction of Europe since the end of the Second World War. Although today's crisis is serious it is not as serious as the 1950s when France was engaged in terrible colonial wars, nor as serious as the 1960s when Spain, Italy and Greece were ruled by non-democratic forces. Poverty, especially in backward agricultural regions, was still endemic in many of today's EU member states in the 1970s and in the following decade half of today's Europe languished under Communist dictatorship. France and Germany have taken major decisions that have helped give Europe the extraordinary decades of peace, prosperity, social justice and freedom that today's European citizens enjoy. Will that Franco-German core now slide into disuse or oblivion? It is possible, but both France and Germany are great nations, and have overcome many of the challenges that history poses. And they are likely to do so again. When the European project was first initiated it was to answer the German question. Now there is a wider European question but only France and Germany can fashion an answer.

7

THE VIEW FROM GERMANY – PERSPECTIVES ON THE CRISIS, ITS ORIGIN AND RESOLUTION

IS THE THERAPY GETTING IN THE WAY OF THE CURE?

It is a popular sport to 'project' the problems of the eurozone onto the inactions or perceived actions of others. While the countries accepting various bail-outs – Greece, Ireland, Portugal and Spain – stand accused of being profligate and spending indiscriminately far beyond their means, the euro's strongest economy, Germany, is in the dock for not giving more financial help sooner. Oh well, as we say, beware of a Greek bearing gifts or, to you and me, don't trust your foes!

Had help arrived from Mrs Merkel and her Cabinet colleagues sooner, her 'gifts' would no doubt have been applauded. But the perceived slowness of Germany's reaction to the euro crisis has given rise to concern that Germany is now acting only out of narrow self-interest, offering Trojan-horse solutions to Europe's failing economies. Like a house of cards, one by one, the euro economies are collapsing, or at least look less stable. Germany relies on its exports to these very same failing economies and the July 2012 downgrading by the Moody's rating agency from stable to negative outlook was a wake-up call for Germany's politicians and policy makers.

Germany has withstood the eurozone crisis reasonably well. As a safe haven for eurozone investors who are pulling out of the other failing economies' bond markets, the cost it pays on its debt is at an all-time low. The private sector's refinancing rates are also historically low, thus stimulating investment and domestic demand. With investors keen to move their money out of the eurozone, the euro exchange rate has depreciated, thereby giving a boost to German exports outside of the eurozone. Yet without wider EU growth German economic performance has suffered. Germany's export-based economy needs other EU member states to import German products and services to maintain profit levels for German firms. Yet the insistence from Berlin that countries should downsize their economies and become more German has the effect of cutting overall EU growth and hence German export-dependent growth. Germany saw a considerable slowdown in 2012 as many eurozone countries contracted. As a result, German GDP fell by 0.7% in the last quarter of 2012 and forecasts were revised sharply downwards with both the IMF and the Bundesbank estimating German growth in 2013 to be a miserable 0.3%. Uncertainty about the prospects of crisis-hit countries within the EU was a major reason for the downward revision. Although eurozone confidence improved as GDP in the second quarter of 2013 grew at 0.7% after just 0.1% in the first quarter, the fastest for a year, the growth was mainly through greater consumer and government spending. Many countries in the eurozone contracted further in the second quarter. And though the region as a whole grew by 0.3% in the second quarter after six quarters of decline, this was mainly because of stronger than expected growth in countries like Germany and France, while Spain, Italy, Ireland and Greece – among others – saw further declines. Forecasts may be revised upwards again but the recent trends do not suggest that the eurozone is out of the woods yet.

How are we to view Germany's actions? In the faculty of economics at the University of Munich, Professor Hans-Werner Sinn, also President of the IFO Institute, has built a reputation as one of Germany's leading economists. A supply-side economist, he has argued for the importance of fundamental market economy reforms and rejected policies that simply aim to raise demand. In 2007 MIT Press published his book *Can Germany Be Saved?*, a reworking in English of his 2003 bestseller *Ist Deutschland noch zu retten?*, which has notched up sales of over 100,000 copies. Professor Sinn is well known to be critical of the workings of the eurozone and the large amounts of money that the Bundesbank has been forced to lend through the mechanics of the refinancing system to the central banks of the peripheral countries. This lending, he points out, is crowding out private credit in non-peripheral countries, because the ECB rates undercut the market. He has, of course, published extensively and represents a particular view in the debate currently taking place in Germany.

There are two ways, goes the German thinking, of dealing with the crisis. One is trying to calm the markets by throwing more money into the rescue operation through the European Stability Mechanism (ESM) and other mechanisms that might be available. Yields would then come down, allowing the crisis to come to an end. The second theory, which is referred to by Professor Sinn as the 'bottomless pit' theory and in which he is a firm believer, contends that there are structural imbalances that will not go away and that by providing funds you inevitably take over from the markets and end up throwing good money after bad. So in his view support for Greece, for example, should stop.

Sinn estimates that a total sum of public funds of €1.5trn has been thrown at the money markets, through various government, EU and IMF institutions and in particular the ECB target system. If you add the new ESM fund that has been set up, the figures in his calculations go up to some €2.2trn. With other countries now also needing support the actual lending will increase beyond the €1.5trn. The belief is that these countries still have large public and, in particular, external deficits, and as long as you finance them they will not be properly tackled at source.

According to this view, the main problem in the crisis countries is that they have become very expensive, as wages are high in relation to their productivity. The concern here is that it is the general price level that determines a country's competitiveness and the problem for many of the crisis countries is that for some years now their inflation rates have been higher than the average for Europe.

Wage rises have of course contributed to this and that, Sinn says, is the main problem. Given that prices are sticky and not on the way down, a big realignment of exchange rates needs to happen to get us back onto a more even economic foundation. Although wages have come down in the periphery economies recently, the improvement in unit labour costs may in fact be more of a reflection of an improvement in productivity, as jobs have been cut back substantially without a real wage cost adjustment. Some austerity measures such as VAT and tax increases have also contributed to pushing prices up since the crisis so the internal devaluation that is needed proceeds more slowly than it would otherwise. Goldman Sachs calculates that Greece needs to lower its prices by 30% and Portugal by 35% to restore competitiveness. Even France needs to lower its prices by 20%. There is an argument that countries like Greece should leave the euro temporarily, devalue and then come back in again at a lower exchange rate.

But of course things can never work as simply as that. If a country leaves the euro because the single monetary policy is not right for it, and inflation is too high because of the structure of the economy, you would have to assume that interest rates will be higher in the period they are out of the euro before falling again when the country opts back in. To prevent hyperinflation surfacing because of devaluation and the need to keep printing money to keep the banks afloat and the monetary system going, you would need temporary capital controls, strict rules on the central bank limiting how much money is printed and a general willingness to keep inflation under control. You would also need massive sums of IMF money to be injected to recapitalise and stabilise the banking system. This is not a risk- or cost-free option by any means.

The idea is similar to that put forward by Roger Bootle of Capital Economics which won him and his team the £250,000 Wolfson Economics Prize, awarded for the best plan for dealing with member states leaving the eurozone. The plan suggested an exiting member should introduce a new currency and default on a large part of its debts. It concluded that the net effect would be positive for growth and prosperity. The Bootle plan also recommended keeping the euro for small transactions for a short period after exit, and a strict regime of inflation targeting and tough fiscal rules monitored by independent experts. Bootle and his team want key officials to meet in secret one month before the exit is publicly announced to agree on the details. Eurozone partners and international organisations would then be informed three days before. Tough medicine for tough times is required.

Sinn thinks Europe should be somewhere between a Bretton Woods-style regime of fixed exchange rates and a single currency – in fact more Bretton Woods than single currency, with currencies allowed to have stable rates against each other but also the flexibility to enter and leave the system, therefore maintaining separate identities. Once the realignment has happened, they should be allowed to return. This mechanism might mean that structural reforms are avoided, and those would need to be addressed, but Sinn holds little hope of the EU really being able to enforce the structural changes attached as conditions to the bail-outs.

But it is generally agreed that if the outcome of one or more countries leaving the euro is that the entire currency breaks up, Germany will lose a great deal. Finding a solution is in everyone's interests, Germany's too. Estimates of the direct cost of euro failure have ranged from €150bn to €1trn and would vary hugely depending on how the exit was carried out. However, these estimates again do not count the indirect costs of possible contagion; they tend to be narrowly focused on what lenders may get back, which is not presenting the right picture. The Institute of International Finance, the global association of banks that represented private lenders to Greece when nego-tiating the second bail-out, took these indirect effects into account when it calculated in February that the total cost of a Greek exit would be a minimum of

€1trn, and that €700bn of that would be needed to prop up other troubled European economies, because the exit would trigger an even deeper decline in European GDP.

I agree with the 'Numbers Guy' of the *Wall Street Journal,* who says that the costs of a Greek exit are incalculable and it would surely not be in Germany's interests to sustain losses of €90bn or more. The most sensible and sustainable solution is for Germany to allow Greece to write off its debt as this is clearly the least costly option for all. The sooner it is realised that Greek and other periphery debt is unsustainable the less the cost to the eurozone.

What is more worrying is that a piecemeal exit from the euro of defaulting countries would 'spook' the markets and lead to greater losses. For those in Germany who would like to see crisis countries exiting the euro, the crisis countries would need to exit together, in an orderly fashion, to minimise damage.

Another worry for the Germans is the proposed move to a banking union. The truth is that there is still remarkably little understanding of what it means. An integrated banking system with common supervision is something European nations were moving to anyway. However, what would clearly be unacceptable to the Germans is a banking union that ends up redistributing money from the better-run countries, such as Germany, to crisis countries that cannot get their act together. There is still a huge overhang of banking sector private debt in Europe in addition to government debt which the banks now hold. A considerable amount of this debt must be 'toxic', unlikely ever to be repaid.

Businesses in Germany are worried about the implications of a euro break-up as it could lead to a serious deterioration in Germany's relative competitiveness – if it is left nursing a strong currency that was hitherto dragged down by weaker and unproductive countries – and could in fact wipe out an awful lot of companies' profits, spelling the end of Germany's leadership position in the economic, and inevitably also political, sphere in Europe. Germans still remember the cost of reunification when just ten years ago the country was famously labelled by *The Economist* as 'the sick man of Europe'.

At a Königswinter economic conference, I recall German representatives bemoaning the lack of entrepreneurship and innovation in the German economy. At the time, the UK economy still had a healthy growth rate and our new research and development (R&D) tax credit regime was cutting the cost of R&D and encouraging investment in research activities, which the Germans envied. Our tertiary education system was also looked at with admiration and there was a lot of bemoaning the lack of a modern industrial strategy in Germany. How things have turned around – Germany is now referred to as the 'strong man' in Europe.

The Germans talk of the current time as a return to what they called the '*Wirtschaftswunder*' of the 1950s, which they have now redefined and re-claimed as the new 'economic miracle'. The premise is success based on an effective market economy, properly regulated to ensure competition but with institutions that guarantee social stability by providing a proper safety net. The then Deputy Finance Minister, Steffen Kampeter, explained at a gathering in London that this basically means that Germany has retained most elements of the social market economy while allowing many decisions to be made jointly by employers and workers' representatives. What has emerged is a treaty between the various social partners – government, firms and workers – which has encouraged the move to a considerably more flexible labour market than the one of the 1970s, '80s and '90s. The example, often quoted, is the way in which workers were kept on during the banking crisis by a part-time payment scheme funded by the government, which allowed people to stay employed and be ready to be productive as soon as conditions improved.

Another reason for the German success is the variety of economic structures, with a good fit between smaller, medium and large businesses allowing even medium-sized businesses to become major players internationally, supported by a varied banking structure. There are 2,000 independent private banks, 400 savings banks, 1,000 cooperatives – and a (reducing) number of *Landesbanken,* which encourage regional and local bespoke lending to businesses, in contrast to the rather concentrated banking structure in places like the UK. Because of the way in which these institutions are funded and owned – usually with a very strong local representation and influence – finance to firms continued to flow through the crisis, even though some of the *Länder* banks and some of the larger global financial institutions such as Commerzbank have had their own share of trouble and have been either closed down, merged or downgraded. Indeed, some Germans suggest that Germany got off lightly precisely because it can only claim to have one global bank – Deutsche Bank – and thus has managed by and large to avoid being contaminated by the global banking problems – at least so far.

But how safe is this model? There are two things to bear in mind. First, that much of the competitiveness of the German economy stems not only from Schröder's reforms but also, as discussed, from a significant amount of outsourcing undertaken by German firms that were keen to take advantage of lower costs in countries in eastern Europe and further afield. Polish exports of intermediate goods have shot up, much of it going into German production and then re-exported to places like China. Second, there is a limit to how long wage demands in Germany will stay moderate. Unions are beginning to flex their muscles and some of the deals arranged recently are inflation busting, contributing to higher inflation in time. There is nothing wrong with that. One of the ways in which some of the problems of the eurozone will be solved will be through higher inflation in

Germany relative to other countries, which will, up to a point, rebalance the relative competitiveness of other countries. The truth is that Germany needs a Europe that continues to expand and it may have to pay more to achieve this. The alternative would be very bad for it. Indeed there are people who talk of 'decade cycles' and believe that once this comparative wage advantage goes, Germany will go back to growing as slowly as any really mature country should be expected to grow. And if demand from the eurozone countries remains depressed for long the 'success' of Germany could well soon be a thing of the past. GDP figures for the second quarter of 2013 for the eurozone as a whole suggest that, though the worst for the region may be over, the recovery remains patchy and consumer demand has generally remained depressed across most of the eurozone – including in Germany itself, as shown by poor retail sales figures. Data suggest that in fact bank lending has been declining in most countries for much of 2013. The slowdown in China and other emerging economies means that China will have to rely a lot more on European growth to sustain its export performance. And that may elude it!

SHOULD THE GERMANS BE MORE LIKE THE GREEKS?

So how are the Germans feeling at present? Should the Germans be more like the Greeks? I deliberately ask the question this way round. Many Germans give the impression they would like the rest of Europe to be, well, German. In London in July 2012 Steffen Kampeter said that the Germans are at a loss to understand what they have done wrong. Twelve years ago, the talk was all about convergence in Europe but it wasn't interpreted in the same way everywhere. Clearly, some feel that the Germans decided they could get their economy to work again properly themselves. They have made the structural reforms that have allowed them to be competitive in an environment where wages were much lower in some countries than in Germany. In the other countries, wages rose faster than Germany's, so there was a degree of convergence, but of course the Germans managed to raise productivity considerably – or retained access to low cost bases through serious outsourcing. But the other countries didn't quite focus on their competitiveness and, as Kampeter pointed out: 'What are the countries expecting Germany to do – stop producing?' Good question. I don't think that anyone is suggesting this but what they are suggesting is for the project to continue and for Germany to appreciate (including its academics), how much Germany a) has benefited from it and b) stands to lose both economically and politically if the euro breaks up. It is the main reason that it can't afford to let the project fail; it will eventually have to relax, bend the rules and accept that it will have to bear the main burden for sorting the rest out. German politicians will have to explain this to their electorate and get them on their side. No other option is possible.

GERMANY'S RESPONSES AND ACTIONS

It is time for German policy makers to put their prejudices to one side. Other nations do work hard. The German way is not the only way. The emphasis must be on growth – even in Germany we have seen growth stalling throughout 2012 and 2013. Without growth the problems will intensify – Spanish and Italian debt rescue will be too large even for Germany, so there is an urgency here that has not been appreciated. My fear is that the mid-sized companies, the backbone of the country, which have become very international and have been loyally supported by their willing local banks, will start to suffer too and then the rot will set in. The impact on the other countries will be severe. Speed is of the essence.

In 2013 Merkel faced not only an election but also a difficult constitutional court: the *Bundesverfassungsgericht*. The court looks at the legality of whatever is agreed in principle during the various summits before it endorses any step forward that may require German financial support. The British of course are constantly puzzled by this as they have no similar constitution! Europe is therefore held captive to a messy political arrangement in Germany, delaying much-needed steps to get the economy going. In the meantime, money is moving into Germany with yields at such low or even negative levels that there are suggestions the markets are prepared to take the hit on expectation of a possible exit of Germany from the euro – or alternatively the exit of weak countries from the euro, which would have the same result: a 'German' currency revaluation and hence gains for the holders of those assets.

LOOKING BEYOND THE GERMAN TABLOID PRESS

At a subtler level, are German policy makers aware of these truths but unable to voice them? The German tabloid press may be limiting what can be said publicly for fear of voters' reactions being negative.

Dr Waltraud Schelkle, a senior lecturer in Political Economy at the European Institute and the London School of Economics, provided an idea of the German sentiment towards Greece's predicament, beyond the superficial headlines:

> We now know that Greece was apparently bankrupt upon entry. This can explain why governments, and not only Germany, do not have much patience with Greece any more, in contrast to Portugal. One time offenders are forgiven, serial offenders are a problem in a club that ultimately rests on trust in each other.

The truth is that 'legal process' is hardwired in the German psyche. Merkel herself is believed to have no 'European' vision as such because of her East German background. Helmut Kohl did but Gerhard Schröder, Merkel's predecessor, didn't. He, in fact, saw the EU at the time as being against him and against Germany. Merkel is not wedded to political union either. What she and Jens Weidmann, the current Bundesbank

President and Merkel's former economic advisor, appear to want is more intensive scrutiny of each country's finances and strict controls but no automatic sharing of budgetary resources in emergency situations.

Clearly this position is not sustainable. The Germans are finding it increasingly difficult to keep that image going and are being misunderstood. As a result, the impression they give is the opposite of what perhaps they had intended. They are, after all, seen as wanting increased control of what individual countries are doing and more scrutiny of other countries' budgets before they are presented to their own national parliaments. At the same time they can't offload this responsibility; they seem to be equally suspicious of European institutions. In an article in the *Financial Times* headlined 'Saving the euro: Dinner on the edge of the abyss', Tony Barber wrote that Merkel vetoed the new rescue fund coming under EU auspices, which would also incidentally have increased the powers of the Commission. Something had to give. Merkel instead accepted the proposal for a structural finance vehicle which became the €500bn European Financial Stability Facility – an extra €250bn made available by the IMF – with loans from it to any country being based on bilateral country agreements. Nevertheless, in reality with this came a form of 'mutualisation' of finances, which originally the Germans had resisted. So, in the process, despite original intentions, the Germans have been increasingly taking a disproportionate (in their minds) share of the financial burden. They are facing a similar situation with the European

Stability Mechanism debate and what its responsibilities should be. There seems to be a problem at every step – subject to the aforementioned constitutional court – but with every crisis Germany is being pushed kicking and screaming closer to 'burden sharing' and ultimately a full risk-sharing mechanism that transfers funds from Germany to the periphery.

POLITICAL LEADERSHIP AND THE GERMAN PSYCHE

Senior government officials in Germany insist that the crisis in the euro was 'the number one issue' for the government and for business. They argue that countries have invested much political capital in the euro and want to look after their investment. They were pleased with the bright review the IMF gave them in July 2012, and felt justified in their pursuit of a very solid economic and financial policy. Germany will, as far as they are concerned, remain in the general meaning of the term a 'safe haven' and they proclaim that it will continue to be 'a very responsible player in the eurozone'.

But the Moody's Investors Services decision to change Germany's AAA sovereign ratings on 23 July 2012 from stable to negative outlook ruffled feathers. German officials[†] said:

> We have taken note, the risks that Moody's looks at are nothing new, they zoom in on short-term risks but

---

† Interview with high-ranking officials from the German Federal Ministry of Economics and Technology (July 2012).

disregard the long-term potential for stabilisation. In the long term we believe there are a number of measures and instruments that will lead to a sustainable stability of the eurozone.

Austerity, they said, was not the issue for German policy makers:

This is not about the Bundesbank and the Germans having a propensity towards austerity, that is missing the point. It is about achieving a sustainable solution; we need checks and balances in order to contain the situation so that we can all return to a more sensible path in the future.

It appears that German policy makers' response has been methodically stitched together. They said:

In Brussels and in the EU, we had to take steps to put instruments and agreements in place. These helped us step by step to contain the crisis. We came to a much more granular understanding of the crisis and a much more granular way of responding to it.

Tellingly they said they were not ruling out the need for a growth stimulus in the future and claimed that youth unemployment would be a focus.

There is enough money, there is enough liquidity in Europe. What we now need to do is to find useful

projects to invest in and that is the more difficult part.
Give us a good project in Greece.

At its core the German political class considers itself
pro-Europe and wants the eurozone to succeed. They
have in their bones the recent history of German reunification where more or less similar steps had to be
taken. Officials are keen to emphasise that there is no
deep-rooted hostility towards Greece and that Greece is
so much a part of Europe that they would do whatever
it takes to get it back on a sound financial footing.

Indeed, commentators seem to have overlooked the
fact that Germany has a lot of Greeks living there.

There is a fabric of Greeks in Germany who have
blended well, so there is no issue. For us Greece is part
of Europe.

It will be interesting to see how things turn out in
practice. At the time of writing the Greek issue still
hangs in the balance and Germany will play a crucial
role in any decision. There is considerable speculation
as to whether Merkel, at the head of a new coalition
after her win in the September 2013 German elections,
will grasp the nettle and soften her stance towards
Greece and the other periphery countries. That would
require her finally to accept publicly what I suspect
she believes privately already, that in Greece, but also
in many other countries in Europe, the debt is unsustainable and that Germany will just have to shoulder

much of the financial burden to finally resolve the debt crisis. But I suspect that the Germans must be wondering whether, if we knew then what we know now, the euro project would have gone ahead at all. Most depressing is to reflect on how expectations have been dashed – only a few years ago Europe's leaders set out the Lisbon agenda, designed to make Europe the most dynamic economy in the world. In fact, the opposite has happened.

8

THE SPANISH PERSPECTIVE – THE VIEW FROM MADRID

On the other side of the Mediterranean, Spain was considered to have done well by joining the euro and its banking system appeared unscathed by the financial crisis. Tight central bank regulation that did not allow the development of off-balance-sheet assets had prevented Spanish banks from indulging in the type of behaviour that exposed so many banks to the risks of 'exotic' products such as derivatives. The Spanish central bank was hailed as an example of best practice. Well, look where they are now.

Consider these mid-2012 headlines when the crisis hit:

Spain in crisis talks with Germany over €300bn bail-out – Luis de Guindos to meet Germany's Wolfgang Schäuble over spiralling bond yields in eurozone's fourth biggest economy (*The Guardian*, 23 July)

Spain crisis worsens as confidence ebbs – bond markets look like they have lost confidence in Spain (*Financial Times*, 23 July)

> Euro exit beats begging bowl, says Spanish elder
> statesman – the regional leader of Asturias in Spain
> has become the country's first major figure to call for
> a radical change of strategy and exit from the euro,
> unless monetary union is fundamentally reformed.
> (*Daily Telegraph*, 26 June)

Recent economic history explains the critical need for help at that stage. In Spain, like in other periphery countries, the very low interest rates that came with the formation of the euro were completely inappropriate for the country. They encouraged huge credit expansion by domestic banks, especially in construction, and a house-building boom followed which lasted for many years. Capital flows into the country, in the form of foreign financial institutions providing cheap loans or funds moving in to get a high return, exacerbated this. And it wasn't just big overseas investors. The UK's television schedules were full of programmes showing UK homeowners how they could cash in by buying a Spanish property with their spare equity.

In July 2012 Alistair Darling, the UK Chancellor during the financial crisis, said that at the time

> the striking thing about Spain was that everywhere
> you went you saw tower cranes over building sites that
> were half finished. I thought, who on earth was paying
> for all this stuff? We know now who was paying for
> it. Equally, like everyone else I have friends in Spain
> with Spanish houses which you can't sell now for

love nor money because the property prices have just
collapsed. You can't shift these houses and there must
be substantial problems there.

His words proved prophetic; the doom-laden headlines appeared within days of our conversation.

But it wasn't just housing that fuelled Spain's debt
problems. Consumer credit also became more abun-
dant and Spanish competitiveness started to suffer as
many goods started coming in from abroad. Spanish
goods' share in total export markets seemed to hold
up but imports soared and the balance of payments
deteriorated. But as in Greece and Portugal, nobody
took notice, and certainly not the sovereign credit
agencies. In the process, Spain made its social welfare
system one of the most generous in Europe, indulged
in a big expansion of the tertiary education system
and embarked on a huge infrastructure programme,
not all of it particularly productive. Because the going
was good, very little attention was paid to structural
reforms which should have provided the basis for
sustainable growth. When the crisis hit, Spain, too,
found itself without the necessary hinterland and
productivity improvement that might have helped.

Spain's structural problems were clearly significant.
Because regional governments are particularly strong
and have their own assemblies and municipalities that
need to be supported, Spain has a big bureaucracy,
making cutting the size of the public sector particularly
difficult. And even in the best years, Spain had one of

the highest, if not the highest, unemployment rates in Europe, which rarely came down below 11%. Its strict employment rules for permanent employees meant that many people actually worked in the shadow sector without being officially employed. Employers would hire people on short-term contracts, often foreign workers; indeed, more than three million foreigners from Latin America, north Africa and from eastern Europe and beyond came to Spain in the long boom years of 1998–2008 (nearly 400,000 Brits have moved there to retire). By March 2012, the unemployment rate in Spain had reached 24.1%, twice the eurozone average. For those under the age of twenty-five, unemployment was over 50%. Employees on short-term contracts accounted for 25% of the total workforce.

So what about the Spanish 'miracle'? Interestingly, until recently there was no doubt that the euro had been fantastic. The economy grew very fast in the early years and it is only now that things are beginning to turn that opinions are changing.

The crisis in Spain appeared to mirror that of the early months of the crisis in Greece and the political squabbles that ensued. Bickering started straight away. Francisco Álvarez Cascos, the former President of the Asturias region and Secretary-General of Spain's ruling party, was particularly virulent, accusing Prime Minister Rajoy of humiliating the nation by going around Europe with a begging bowl. He apparently accused the government of being 'utterly incompetent', and warned of the danger of being thrown out of the euro. Recent experiences in Europe point to how quickly these seeds of discontent can grow.

The spotlight on Spain's banks only came about after the dust from the financial crisis appeared to have settled and it was only because the house-building boom came to an abrupt halt a couple of years ago that the problems of the banking sectors have come to the fore. It is astonishing really as it was just over two years ago, in the summer of 2011, that Bankia, a bank that was brought together through the merger of a number of regional mort-gage banks, had an initial public offering that went very well but soon started to feel hugely overvalued when it was realised how many of the loans were in fact underperforming. The management of Bankia itself came under scrutiny, including the ex-President Rodrigo Rato, who was Managing Director of the IMF between June 2004 and October 2007.

Given the banking crisis in Spain it became clear that a loan to recapitalise the banks was necessary. On 9 June 2012, the IMF's Managing Director, Christine Lagarde, supported the intention by the eurozone to provide up to €100bn (£846m) to meet the Spanish banks' capital needs. The IMF also offered to moni-tor the implementation of the package of support. But more confirmation of this came on 13 June 2012 just as I was arriving in Madrid to research this book. The deal had been touch and go and the details of the loan had still not been disclosed at that stage. But clearly, given that Spain is the fourth largest country in the eurozone, the Spanish government had no wish to be put in the same bracket as the other periphery countries, Ireland, Portugal and Greece, which had gone cap in hand to their partners in Europe and the IMF to get bail-outs – and without which they would not have been able to meet their sovereign debt obligations. Spain held off until it managed to get a deal that was sold as being specifically for the banks that were in trouble because of the bad loans that had accumulated during a long house-building boom that went badly sour. Arguably Spain should have done something earlier to clean up the banks or at least get a handle on the extent of the problem but the various stress tests done by the national authorities seemed not to reveal the full extent of the problems suffered by the specialist mortgage lenders.

The deal was another classic example of political confusion and prevarication, and bodes ill for any sort of political union in the eurozone in the future. With no fiscal conditions attached it was not described as a bail-out. This allowed the government to claim that Spain was very different to the other periphery countries that had already been forced to seek bail-outs.

That bank bail-out, however, had not fooled the markets despite some initial relief that at least a full-scale banking crisis had been averted. There is no doubt that the developing banking crisis in Spain, engulfing most though not all banks – the largest ones such as Santander and BBVA were not expected to draw any money from the loan facility – had to be addressed as it was threatening to affect the banking sector all across Europe. The markets were spooked by the process through which the bank recapitalisation would happen – initially through Spain's own bank rescue fund, which would add to the government debt. If permanent, this would result in the debt-to-GDP ratio rising from 80% to nearer 90% depending on how much of the €100bn was in the end needed. Reflecting these concerns, Spanish bond yields were pushed up again after the initial relief.

The measure of contagion that was already in the system meant that attention then quickly turned to Italy, even though on the surface it is in a much better shape, with a cleaner banking system and no house-building boom. Nevertheless investors became increasingly concerned that Italy would soon follow suit as it has the biggest debt-to-GDP ratio outside Greece in the eurozone and has enjoyed very little growth in its economy for years. It also became obvious that if the problems were confined to Portugal, Ireland and Greece the European Financial Stability Facility cushion was sufficient but if Spain, let alone Italy, were added then the European safety net would just not be big enough to provide the amount of support that might be needed.

The upshot of this, together with pressure from Italy, Spain and France under the new President, François Hollande, was that the European summit on 28 June 2012 had to revisit this again. An agreement with Chancellor Merkel began to take shape. Once a single bank regulator was in place, any recapitalisation money would be given directly to the banks via the European Stability Mechanism (ESM) and therefore would not be added to the country's debt. The same would happen if Italy needed some assistance in the future. Ireland has also made noises to convert sovereign debt used to recapitalise its banks into ESM assistance, once the regulator is in place, and there is a possibility that Greece, 'if it behaves', may benefit too. In the intervening period nevertheless, and until a single eurozone regulator is established, any assistance would still temporarily add to the government's debt.

The 9 July 2012 European finance ministers' meeting ratified the Spanish deal and made €30bn of funding available to Spain by the end of the month as part of the €100bn package (the actual sum requested by Spain in October 2012 amounted to €39.5bn after an independent review of its banks). For a while, the markets reacted favourably and yields dropped. But, of course, as with everything else it looked for a while as if the agreement was not rock solid. The German Constitutional Court had difficulty with it, the Finns and the Dutch interpreted it differently and the initial positive mood quickly evaporated. There was also continued confusion as to what was meant by rushed talks of creating a banking union, which created a further area of uncertainty. Spain was teetering on the edge of financial disaster which could have torn the single currency apart. Analysts said at the time that

Spain's huge economy was at a 'tipping point' and would inevitably need international aid. Later in July, at a London conference, ECB Governor Mario Draghi said that the ECB would do what it takes to support Spain and the eurozone in general – and he reiterated that in early August after the monthly ECB board meeting. But what has it all meant for Spain? There is no doubt that trust in the banking sector and in the politicians has suffered – and further banking and political scandals brought to light in 2013, even involving the Prime Minister, only made matters worse. The continued absence of a Europe-wide deposit guarantee scheme remains a worry for bank depositors. But the help from Europe has at least had the desired effect of calming the markets and lowering Spanish yields which were as dangerously high as those that triggered proper bail-outs for smaller 'periphery' countries. The problem has not gone away as there is still the fallout from the earlier over-expansion in lending, particularly to the property sector, to deal with but at least the country has returned to some form of relative calm though economic growth has failed to materialise. Unemployment in mid-2013 stood at over 26%, just below that of the worst eurozone performer, Greece. But is this sustainable for what is the fourth largest country in the eurozone? And had the men who had presided over the initial Spanish boom and excessive borrowing from 1996 to 2004 learned any lessons?

Spaniards have no wish to leave the euro, which they see as having given them a lot of benefits in the past, and they would be prepared to cede even more sovereignty if necessary to preserve their place in the EU and the eurozone. Talk of banking union, whatever that might mean in the end, which requires giving up the right to an independent fiscal policy, does not seem to concern '*el hombre de la calle*', nor Spain's politicians. But how long will that last?

Why were there no additional conditions for Spain of the type others had to agree to? Part of this is politics and part for show. Spain is a big economy. Its leaders did not want to be seen as submitting to the regime that had been imposed on Greece, Ireland and Portugal. Nor did the rest of the eurozone wish to see support for Spain labelled as the same form of bail-out for fear it would exhaust the collective resources for financial rescues and rattle the markets further. In addition, Spain had already made a start in implementing reforms and it had been serious about cutting its deficit. But, as it became evident that the government would not meet its 3% deficit target in 2013 in line with the requirements of the Stability and Growth Pact, which was extended to 2014, reforms are long overdue. In late May 2013 the deadline was shifted by a further two years to 2016, the longest given to any non-bail-out EU country, in recognition of the difficulties that Spain was having in controlling its finances. Given that the deficit for 2012 was 7%, much higher than earlier forecasts, and the expectation for 2013 is for it to have reduced only slightly to 6.5%, this makes sense and suggests a long-awaited recognition that austerity in itself has unintended consequences that might lead at times to difficulties in meeting deficit targets if economies contract significantly. This approach was also applied to other non-bail-out countries like France, which also saw an extension in their targets, but the longest any country has to meet those targets is until 2015. Different rules of course apply for countries struggling under bail-out conditions. In reality, there were conditions attached to the conduct of the banking sectors which effectively gave powers over to the IMF and the troika – and it soon became obvious that there were implicit conditions attached to the whole fiscal conduct of the authorities as well, wrapped up in European guidelines on economic governance.

It now, therefore, appears that the mismanagement and lax regulation in the banking sector had a severe impact upon the wider economy and the population, with the Spaniards unveiling €65bn austerity measures in the week that the first tranche of funding from the EU for bank recapitalisation was made available. The measures were to take effect over the deficit reduction period and included a cut in unemployment benefits, a freeze of civil service pay, later retirement, and a plan to privatise railways, ports and airports. The measures also increased taxes, both VAT and on corporations, reduced some industrial subsidies and promised to streamline public corporations and improve public sector efficiency. There were more austerity measures in the 2013 budget unveiled in late September. Not surprisingly the economy, which was likely to contract in both 2012 and 2013 anyway, declined by 1.4% in 2012.

So Rajoy's claim that there were no austerity conditions attached to the bank bail-out plan now sounds hollow – and there was, as proven later, worse to come. The miners were striking as Rajoy presented his measures in Parliament. When King Juan Carlos appeared in an embarrassing photo while on a luxury safari in Africa, it reminded everyone that the Europe of the rich, of oligarchs and royals, remains untouched by the crisis – and that fuels continued resentment and unrest.

In effect Spain joined Greece, Ireland, Portugal and Cyprus in asking for bail-outs, even if these requests were presented in different forms to save face. The situation in Italy looked pretty fragile, too, given its high debt-to-GDP ratio and came under pressure from the markets a number of times in the following twelve months despite a reasonably healthy deficit position. A club of three troubled euro countries had by late 2012 become, for all intents and purposes, a club of five. A small periphery country problem had evolved into a serious eurozone issue, requiring a radically different approach – but do the European leaders 'get it'?

Well, not on the evidence of the positive noises made recently about how the situation in Spain is improving when the fundamentals actually haven't shifted all that much. The *Daily Telegraph*'s assistant editor, discussing the latest IMF projections for Spain, argued in May 2013 that a Spanish debt restructuring was inevitable and although the ECB had promised to print money and counter speculators, and the country's sovereign bond yields had fallen sharply since Draghi's announcement of his 'outright monetary transactions' programme, he believed that in the end Spain's solvency problem would not be covered by throwing huge amounts of liquidity at it.

9

WHY BRITAIN MAY LEAVE EUROPE
BEFORE GREECE QUITS THE EURO

In the Oscar-winning film *The Iron Lady*, Meryl Streep portrays a ranting Mrs Thatcher. Her target: a hapless Geoffrey Howe. If he wants to be pro-European, she shouts, why doesn't he go off to France? It is an utterly made-up scene and, like so many historical howlers in the film, distorts the deeper reasons for the drift to Euroscepticism that began in the 1980s and is now utterly dominant in British politics.

My own experiences of being in the thick of it were thankfully not as polarised as the Thatcher film, but as Joint Head of the Government Economic Service in 2008/9, when the global financial crisis hit, I sat on the officials group of the newly formed National Economic Council, an advisory Cabinet committee run by the then Prime Minister, Gordon Brown, and the Chancellor, Alistair Darling. We worked round the clock, across departments at a senior level, devising measures and economic policy tools to resolve the economic problems created by the collapse of Lehman

Brothers. That moment is now one of the most important landmarks in recent political history and one that
historians will dwell on for many years to come. In the
UK we worked 'unitedly', as those famous statesmen of
the past have urged politicians to do in times of crisis.

UNDERSTANDING BRITAIN'S CURRENT EUROSCEPTICISM

In 1942, Churchill submitted a memo to Cabinet
colleagues in which he declared:

> Hard as it is to say now, I trust that the European
> family may act unitedly as one under a Council of
> Europe. I look forward to a United States of Europe in
> which the barriers between the nations will be greatly
> minimised and unrestricted travel will be possible.

No British politician today would dare come close to
making the same remarks. Why?

The main reason is economic. In the period after
the 1957 Treaty of Rome, the Common Market states
were seen to be growing much faster than the UK.
They were thus an example to follow. The Thatcher
years were a decade of catch-up, not some kind of
economic revolution. But since 1990, those on a par
with Britain in the EU have fallen behind in terms
of growth.

So for British economic policy makers, Europe was a
compelling example to follow in the 1960s and 1970s.
Even into the 1980s, UK growth rates compared unfa-
vourably with those of the main EC players. By the

1990s, however, it was Britain that outperformed its main EU rivals, especially Germany, which had taken on the deadweight of a merger with a bankrupt East German economy, the impact of which has still not worked through.

Moreover, by the 1990s, the US economy was powering ahead as Silicon Valley, universities and mass immigration allowed America to set a cracking pace of growth, especially during the Clinton era. The rise of British Euroscepticism coincides almost precisely with the end of British inferiority in relation to mainland Europe's better economic performance from 1950 to 1985.

This also coincided with efforts in Brussels to promote the EU as a region with the institutions of statehood – a parliament, an executive, foreign and military policies, a single currency, a constitution, a flag and an anthem. But – at present at any rate – the EU is not a state. Fewer than 7% of laws passed by the UK Parliament stem from the EU, according to surveys by the House of Commons Library. The EU budget is just 1% of EU gross national income, 85% of which goes back to member states as agricultural and regional development subsidies.

But these realities are, as far as I can see, lost in Britain, where most of the media coverage would seem to suggest that membership and support of the EEC, EC and EU have always been contested. And yet there were periods of strong European support. After 1945, it was the Conservative Party that was the European party. Churchill (1940–55), Macmillan (1957–63) and Heath (1965–75) were three party leaders, then Prime Ministers, who supported supranational European institution building and integration.

Conservative ministers up to the late 1980s appear, in large majority, to have been consistently pro-European. Labour, in contrast, was the Eurosceptic party. In 1950, the Labour government rejected joining the Coal and Steel Community. In 1962, the Labour leader, Hugh Gaitskell, said that to join the EEC was to 'abandon 1,000 years of history'. In 1972, the majority of Labour MPs voted against entry into the EEC and in 1983, Labour's election manifesto included a pledge to withdraw from the EEC.

Why did Labour become pro-EU under Tony Blair? His own and, it appears, Gordon Brown's personal convictions were pro-EU. But was it also on the basis of 'my enemy's enemy is my friend' that Labour moved? Margaret Thatcher, having pioneered the Single European Act and agreed to a quadrupling of the UK contribution to the EU budget (£654m in 1984 increased to £2.5bn in 1990 despite her claiming to have won her money back!), reacted very strongly to a speech in favour of social rights and trade union power made by Jacques Delors to the Trades Union Congress in 1988. This was the most important intervention by a European in the post-war debate in Britain. It utterly altered the balance between Conservatives and Labour. Delors was an austere, fiscally prudent, pro-business, Catholic social activist. Yet somehow a moderate, cautious speech about social Europe in 1988 transformed the political balance of the Europe question inside Britain.

It made the trade unions and the Labour Party see virtues in European integration they had not noticed before. It drove Mrs Thatcher and the growing Conservative anti-union groups wild with rage. Mrs Thatcher denounced Europe as 'introducing socialism by the back door'. Helmut Kohl and other EC Conservatives might have been surprised at this concept of Europe, as would have been many on the French left who regarded Europe and Jacques Delors as a neo-liberal conspiracy intent on abolishing national economic controls and strengthening pro-business competition. Thus from 1990 onwards, and especially after Britain's forced exit from the ERM in 1992, the British right became more and more hostile to the EU and the Labour Party more broadly positive, at least in the fifteen years of John Smith's (1992–4) and Tony Blair's (1994–2007) leadership.

This rejection of social Europe spread across business groups that hitherto had been pro-European. Every modest social regulation risked being portrayed as a Brussels diktat designed to destroy British business. It also coincided with the decline in growth of comparative major EU states. A consensus emerged that the Anglo-Saxon, pro-market 'Atlantic model' also favoured in the US was preferable to the more controlled and regulated Brussels–Rhine socio-economic model. High levels of unemployment in

Germany and France by the end of the 1990s, while unemployment was going down in Britain, appeared to confirm that viewpoint.

Unlike the Conservatives of the 1950s, 1960s, 1970s and even up to 1985, senior Labour ministers avoided making a pro-European case in their political narratives. Tony Blair made some good speeches in support of European integration, but he made them on the continent, rarely if ever in Britain. One of the first acts of Jack Straw as Foreign Secretary was to abolish an inter-ministerial EU coordinating committee which was meant to make the government as a whole more Europe-conscious.

After coming to power, a pro-EU and pro-euro Prime Minister Tony Blair clearly knew, as all Labour politicians did, that to get euro entry agreed via a referendum, which all parties had promised, would have been impossible. Had Blair plunged Britain into a Europe referendum in the first period of his premiership there would have been three consequences. First, the Conservative Party would have sprung back to life in a campaign against the single currency. Second, the right-wing press would have reverted to out-and-out hostility against Labour on the issue of a euro referendum. Third, a good block of Labour MPs would have campaigned against the euro entry. Backed by key advisors like Ed Balls, who regularly briefed against the euro, long-standing Eurosceptics within the Labour Party felt marginalised by Labour's pro-Europeanism articulated first by Neil Kinnock and John Smith, and then made full-throated New Labour policy by Blair, Peter Mandelson, Robin Cook and Giles Radice.

But Blair wanted Britain to be seen as taking the euro seriously. John Major had described the idea of the euro's creation as 'being as quaint as a rain dance'. From 1950 onwards Britain had always insisted that the different stages of European construction could not and therefore would not happen. James Callaghan, the Labour Prime Minister before Blair, had tried in 1978 to enlist Jimmy Carter to stop the European Monetary System proposed by Valéry Giscard d'Estaing and Helmut Schmidt from coming into being.

The Treasury, led by Gordon Brown and Ed Balls, was a focus of anti-Brussels sentiment in any case. Retiring Cabinet Secretary Sir Gus O'Donnell, in a valedictory appearance in front of the Commons Treasury Select Committee in late 2010, commented that he had saved Britain from the euro. But however independent was the research and analysis linked to the five economic tests set by Gordon Brown as Chancellor to decide the virtues or otherwise of possible UK entry, it was clear at the time across government, even among pro-euro and pro-EU ministers, that there was never any serious sense that eurozone entry was on the cards. It was never going to happen and the debate today has moved on – not from British entry into Europe but rather British exit from Europe. The UK Independence Party (UKIP), fiercely anti-European and led by MEP Nigel Farage, has thrived as a result, attracting many Conservative votes.

WHY THE EU STILL DIVIDES UK PARTIES

Unlike France, Germany, the Netherlands, Italy, or Spain where there was large political consensus about Europe, the EU is a divisive, difficult topic for the ruling parties in Britain.

Visionaries like Churchill may have dreamed of a United States of Europe in 1942 but there has never been the imperative in the UK that drove a de Gaulle and an Adenauer, or those with wartime memories like Mitterrand or Kohl, to establish something that would make any future war in Europe impossible.

Charles Grant of the Centre for European Reform points to four reasons for Britain's Euroscepticism. First, history: Britain had a very honourable war while most other European countries didn't and that has set us apart. Second, geography: Britain is at the edge of Europe and that, combined with its history, means that it has traditionally had more global trade flows, investment flows and migration flows than any other country in Europe. Third, economics: from the mid-1990s to 2008 Britain had the most successful economy of any big country in Europe. And fourth: the role of the British media. Of all newspapers sold in Britain, 75% preach Euroscepticsm and many proprietors don't allow their journalists to deviate far from that line. Quoting research by the Oxford academic Tim Garton Ash, Grant confirms that the press, particularly the tabloids, have tended to exaggerate the bad things and not cover the good things about Europe.

But why have the British become even more Eurosceptic? Grant thinks it is because the eurozone crisis has demonstrated the incompetence of eurozone leaders who, according to Grant, are perceived not to be able 'to run a piss-up in a brewery'. This has helped the Eurosceptics develop a new narrative. The old narrative, according to him, was that Europe should be mistrusted as it was becoming an all-conquering superstate, chewing up sovereignty piece by piece. They now have a completely new narrative: the EU is a millstone around one's neck, a slow moving, overregulated, social democratic, monopolistic, slow-growing region. Under this narrative Britain needs to liberate itself and build new dynamic relationships with the rapidly growing emerging markets of Brazil, Russia, India, China and beyond.

So the tone has changed. Rather than grumbling about being in the European Union there is now a concerted push to get out of Europe altogether. The politics of a referendum about Britain and Europe have been firmly placed on the agenda by the British Prime Minister, David Cameron. In July 2009, the Conservative Party withdrew from its long-standing membership of the mainstream centre-right political grouping called the European People's Party (EPP). The EPP groups parties such as Angela Merkel's Christian Democratic Union (CDU), Mariano Rajoy's Union for a Popular Movement (UMP), Spain's *Partido Popular*, and governing centre-right parties in Sweden, Poland and Greece, as well as providing the political home for the Presidents of the European Commission and Council and the majority bloc in the European Parliament.

Instead, David Cameron created a new alliance of populist, nationalist political parties from Poland, Latvia and the Czech Republic. Four years later in a speech in January 2013, Mr Cameron said he wanted an 'In–Out' referendum on Europe. He said that if re-elected in 2015 he would renegotiate a new relationship between Britain and the EU, and in 2017 citizens could decide if the UK stayed in or left the EU. This was the first time that a Conservative Prime Minister had thrown the weight of his office behind the idea of a defining referendum on Britain's relationship with the rest of Europe. Margaret Thatcher denounced referendums as 'a device of dictators and demagogues', but her successor in Downing Street is now officially committed to the idea.

Britain's Foreign Secretary, William Hague, announced that the Foreign Office would launch an 18-month consultation about what was wrong in Britain's relationship with the EU. Everyone – politicians, civil servants, businesses and members of the public – could make their submission to Mr Hague on what competences or powers Britain should seek to repatriate from Brussels. The impact of the collapse of confidence in Europe's economic model, symbolised by the never-ending eurozone crisis, combined with the startling rise of a new European immigrant population in small British towns, let alone big cities, has turned the European question into bread-and-butter politics, on which everyone has a view. And yet despite the general anti-EU mood in the UK, employers have hired eastern European workers whose skills and willingness to work long hours and weekends are preferred to lower-skilled British workers. At the same time the EU has made little progress on the social agenda and the unions' support for the agenda has declined with cheaper European workers seen as a threat. Even the former Labour Prime Minister Gordon Brown had boasted to the Labour Party conference that he would provide 'British jobs for British workers'. He could not keep his promise but appeared to be validating those to the right of Labour who argued that British jobs were being given to non-British workers.

This crisis over jobs, along with the way ministers blame the UK's difficult economic situation on the continuing absence of demand in the eurozone, has inflamed the debate over Europe in the UK.

David Cameron has made clear in private meetings with François Hollande and other EU leaders that, in exchange for Britain's signature on a new Treaty setting up a banking or fiscal Union or any other supranational legal authority, he expects to be granted massive opt-outs and derogations that will abolish many existing EU rules currently applying to Britain. If not, he will threaten a veto. He has some support in that: even the strongest Europhiles agree that Brussels does too much and the bureaucracy of twenty-eight Commissioners and three Presidents (the Council, the

Commission and the Parliament) has left the EU without a clear mission, leadership or purpose.

But the kind of semi-detached relationship that the present Conservative leadership wants with Europe may be too much for the Commission and the other twenty-six member states to offer. So, again, the issue of a British referendum now has high salience in British politics. Charles Grant believes that the chances of Britain being in the EU by the end of the next parliament are no better than 50%.

Labour's official position is to stay in the EU but there are many Labour MPs who have lost the pro-European zeal that the New Labour generation of Tony Blair and Peter Mandelson incarnated from the early 1990s onwards. Hardly any Labour MPs take part in Commons debates on Europe in contrast to the massed ranks of Eurosceptic Conservative MPs on the benches opposite. Labour opposes the financial transaction tax and has criticised the government's sleight-of-hand efforts to support EU bail-outs via an increase in funds to the IMF. Labour ministers opposed most of the social provisions in Europe including the Working Time Directive and the Agency Workers Directive. British trade unions who saw 'Social Europe' as a key reason for supporting the EU in the 1990s are now disappointed and have lost their previous pro-EU enthusiasms.

NO-BAIL-OUT CLAUSE

The no-bail-out clause, now of course breached repeatedly, was the axis on which the euro deal rested. The euro would never have got started if there hadn't been agreement on a no-bail-out clause. It was the reason the Germans accepted it at all.

What the ERM debacle of 1992 did was solidify the UK's reluctance to join the euro. Under two previous Conservative Chancellors – Anthony Barber in the 1970s and Nigel Lawson in the 1980s – high inflation became the norm. Average inflation in the Lawson years was 5.1%. The ERM, although not particularly good for the politicians involved, was at least effective in bringing the UK's inflation rate down. Professor Mundell noted at the time that an exchange rate union linked to the Deutschmark would inevitably lead to inflation rates converging in Europe. After leaving the ERM, the UK benefited from starting again with a much lower inflation rate. Helped also by the downwards adjustment in the exchange rate that followed the exit from the ERM, growth surged. Very high interest rates that had been needed to keep sterling in the ERM eased upon exit. Yet by 1996, sterling had risen to a very high level where it stayed for a decade. With Tony Blair giving the Bank of England independence in 1997 (it remained odd that a Labour rather than a Conservative government took this step) interest rates stayed low. With a high-value, stable pound and low interest rates, the UK enjoyed a long sustained decade of growth from 1997 to 2007.

However, it is necessary to note that the ERM was not a fixed exchange rate system at all. When the UK joined, the band within which exchange rates were allowed to vary for the UK and Spain was 6% and for the others 2.25%. But reflecting exchange rate pressures on that fateful day of 16 September 1992 (known in the UK as 'Black Wednesday'), interest rates had risen very substantially, hitting 12%. The then Chancellor, Norman Lamont, had to tell the Prime Minister that the UK should leave the ERM. A group of ministers, convened by the Prime Minister, rejected his advice and asked him to raise interest rates to 15%. That startling increase was actually never implemented as the UK left the ERM a few hours later. As Norman Lamont puts it in his book, *In Office*:

> Since Black Wednesday the chaos in the market had continued with currencies falling like dominoes, the Lira had been first devalued and then had to withdraw from the ERM. The Portuguese and the Spaniards devalued twice, the Finns, the Swedes and the Norwegians had all floated. The Irish ... were under pressure that was in the end to force devaluation on them too ... The French were prepared to stick to 13% interest rates, which in Britain would have been utterly unacceptable and inappropriate. But the most important point was what was happening to the Deutschmark which soared to unprecedented heights ... The Germans had won their realignment.

The ERM experience should have been a salutary lesson for any new attempts to have exchange rate unions but much of this was ignored during the creation of the euro.

As we have noted, the euro project was essentially a political one, intent on binding Germany into Europe. Britain, however, had devised a new European concept – the opt-out. This had saved John Major from a Cabinet revolt at the time of the Maastricht Treaty when he was given an opt-out from EU social rules. Now the UK had an opt-out from the euro or, more accurately, it was agreed that membership of the euro was not a condition of staying in the EU. Perhaps it should have been. Had Britain left the EU in the mid-1990s we would now know if that would have led to a renaissance of Britain's economy and society or whether, as is the case in Norway and Switzerland, Britain would have to accept most, if not all, EU rules in order to maintain unfettered access to the single market and to allow British citizens the right to free travel and abode in EU member states.

The Germans liked their strong Deutschmark, of course, but were worried about inflation and were proud of their Bundesbank. Yet they were prepared to give all that up though they insisted on a no-bail-out clause in the Maastricht Treaty and also on an independent central bank. With hindsight, it is interesting to consider what was then being sold to the electorate of Germany and France. In Germany, an independent hard-nosed central bank to keep inflation low; in France, Mitterrand went on record during its Maastricht referendum saying that the ECB would be under the control of the politicians, by virtue, one assumes, of the various countries represented on its board. And as Lamont says, this type of dual interpretation among the leaders of the EU and the euro has not gone away. It is visible even today in the disagreements between Merkel and Hollande. The French voters narrowly approved the Maastricht Treaty in a referendum but there was no plebiscite in France specifically on the euro nor did the German public have a chance to vote. Opinion polls at the time suggested that a majority of the population in Germany wanted to keep the Deutschmark up to the last minute. Current polls, if believed, still suggest that they would like to see their own currency back.

According to Lamont, the politicians had no time for economists, who they considered to be just technocrats, so the whole economic argument was not debated in depth – if at all – in many parts of Europe. I remember before the euro notes and coins were introduced giving an after-dinner speech at an international treasurers' event in the Netherlands and sounding a bit sceptical about how the countries in a single currency union would be able to deal with external shocks. I was greeted by a stony, shocked silence – it was probably my worst-received speech ever! The person next to me at the table was from Lisbon – a nice, polite man. But after expressing great surprise at what I had said he proceeded to inform me that in the whole of Portugal there were only two academics who were against the euro and at least one of them was well known to be certifiably mad! I must locate him.

Still, the economists and technocrats had to make

things workable. Jean-Claude Trichet, the pro-euro Governor of France's central bank, believed that the absence of the ability to manipulate exchange rates would force countries to be fiscally prudent and so converge. However, no one was focusing on the way in which the markets would in fact work against that. Many pro-euro economic commentators at the time thought that one of the great advantages of the euro would be the elimination of divergences in sovereign credit risk – rates would fall and the countries would be able to borrow more cheaply, thus encouraging growth. But, in reality, this elimination of an exchange rate risk removes the pressure to be fiscally prudent and encourages imports as the balance of payment constraint disappears.

'GAME, SET AND MATCH' – MAASTRICHT AND THE SOCIAL CHAPTER

At the time of the Maastricht Treaty, Gus O'Donnell, then John Major's press secretary, briefed the UK opt-out as a great success for Major, using the phrase 'Game, set and match', much liked by journalists at the time. Major apparently didn't like this description as it sounded too triumphalist, but O'Donnell thought it an accurate reflection of the conclusions of the negotiations. The UK was expected to reconsider all this at an appropriate time in the future.

The background for us going into the Maastricht negotiations was a particularly difficult one for the UK and for Conservative politicians at the time, as the push was to also have a social chapter attached, which the Conservatives were not prepared to accept. This coloured the UK view of economic and monetary union so, although UK officials participated in the discussion, Europe ended up with a half-baked EMU and the UK had no option but to opt out.

The UK opt-out, though allowing an opt-in at some stage, excluded an obligation towards having to have economic guidelines towards convergence handed down by the Commission or any fines and sanctions associated with the Stability and Growth Pact should the UK not meet the targets towards fiscal consolidation.

When Tony Blair came to power in 1997 with a large majority and with what looked like a mandate to do what he wanted, he, being in favour of joining the euro, decided to look at euro membership again. But Blair had promised a referendum on the euro, as had John Major, prior to the 1997 election. This promise of a plebiscite neutralised the issue of euro entry as a divide between Labour and the Conservatives in 1997. Another pro-euro figure at the time was Peter Mandelson, who later became Blair's Secretary of State for Trade and Industry, though he was subsequently forced to resign. He believed that there would be political advantages in terms of influence in joining and also economic advantages in terms of the reduction in transaction costs and removal of exchange rate risk. But Gordon Brown and Ed Balls were both very nervous of this on mainly economic grounds and the Treasury generally was not very keen either because of the uncertainties. Slowly, the UK moved towards a proper examination of whether it should enter the euro.

THE FIVE ECONOMIC TESTS AND THEIR RELEVANCE TODAY

The invention of the five economic tests in 1997 was a political device that added structure to the decision-making process but actually helped put off making a decision. The handling of this fairly reflected the Blair/Brown dynamics. The criteria of the five economic tests were defined by Gordon Brown, and were used specifically to assess the UK's readiness to join EMU, and therefore to adopt the euro as its official currency. In principle, the tests were distinct from any political decision to join; in reality many people saw them as merely a political device created in order not to join.

So what were the 'five economic tests'?

Cyclical convergence: Are business cycles and economic structures compatible so that we and others could live comfortably with euro interest rates permanently?

Flexibility: If there are problems, is there enough flexibility to deal with them?

Investment: Would joining EMU create better conditions for firms making long-term decisions to invest in Britain?

Financial services: What impact would entry into EMU have on the competitive position of the UK's financial services industry, particularly the City's wholesale markets?

Employment and growth: Essentially, will joining EMU promote higher growth, stability and a lasting increase in jobs?

Not only would the UK have to meet these self-imposed criteria, but it would also need to meet the EU's economic convergence criteria from Maastricht, including two years' membership of the ERM, which the UK had no intention of re-entering.

The 1997 government pledged to assess the tests early in the next parliament (which began in June 2001) and it published an assessment of the five tests in June 2003. The 2003 assessment was led by the Treasury as a tight high-level project with the conclusion that the tests were not met. This assessment ran to around 250 pages and was backed up by eighteen supporting studies, on subjects such as housing, labour market flexibility, and the euro area's monetary and fiscal frameworks.

But what were the conclusions? They were somewhat similar across all five tests.

Cyclical convergence: There had been significant progress on convergence since 1997 but there remained some structural differences, such as the housing market.

Flexibility: UK flexibility had improved but the government could not be confident that it had improved sufficiently.

Investment: Euro membership would undoubtedly increase investment, but only if convergence and flexibility were sufficient.

Financial services: It was concluded that the City of London would benefit from eurozone membership.

Employment and growth: Growth, stability and employment would increase as a result of euro membership, but only if convergence and flexibility were sufficient.

So the conclusion on convergence was doubtful and the verdict was that 'euro membership would increase investment but only if convergence and flexibility were sufficient'. There has been a lot of criticism of how the tests were carried out. The Cabinet was given almost no time to even read, let alone discuss, the details of the 2003 assessment. However, even if not critical to the decision, the process of compiling answers to the tests meant that thought was given in government circles to all the issues surrounding membership. Gus O'Donnell, at the time Head of the Treasury, is adamant that 'the tests were unbiased'. There were differences between Brown and Blair on how to approach the EU question generally but as far as O'Donnell (now Lord O'Donnell) is concerned, the economic concerns won out in the end and the UK stayed outside the euro. My team from the DTI, then headed by Patricia Hewitt, a strong pro-European and euro supporter, contributed evidence looking at the sectoral implications for the UK in the case of membership. And it has stood the test of time. What has clearly happened is that the single currency has been extended, probably wrongly, to countries that cannot in fact converge. In this it is useful, I think, to look at the Irish situation. Irish banks are estimated to have lost at least €100bn, much of it on bad loans to property developers and homeowners made in the midst of the property bubble, which burst around 2007. The situation would have been even worse in the UK if we had entered the euro when it was set up. There was a commitment to review our 'path to convergence' every year but that was soon abandoned.

'EVENTS, DEAR BOY, EVENTS!'

Where does this leave the UK now? The events of the last five years will have convinced many that it was the right decision to stay outside the single currency. Life would have been more difficult if sterling had not been able to depreciate. The UK could even have been forced into seeking a bail-out itself, bringing back memories of 1976 and the secret discussions held between the British government and the IMF in a Mayfair tailor's shop. There are few voices left advocating UK entry into the single currency at any time in the near future. Staying out of the single currency for the current parliament must have been one of the easiest points to agree when coalition policy was being put together.

Yet the course of events creates some real dilemmas for the UK and possibly brings forward the point when the UK will need to decide whether its long-term destiny is to be in closer union with continental Europe or outside it – and possibly indeed outside the EU. If the eurozone was to fall apart, the UK would be affected by the ensuing economic turmoil. If, as is more likely, the eurozone manages to move in steps towards closer fiscal, political and economic union, then the position of those countries outside the eurozone might become more difficult, in terms of the impact they can have on their own futures. They risk the key decisions being taken in advance by eurozone politicians, with the options open to them increasingly being restricted to use of the veto when the legal basis permits. Peter Mandelson has speculated:

> If the eurosceptics have their way, the UK's position in future might be rather like that of a country such as Norway, which is in the European Economic Area but outside the EU – having to abide by rules that they have had no influence in formulating.

Essentially a country with such a status gets a communication from Brussels telling it what has been decided and then has to implement the decision on a 'take-it-or-leave-the-EEA' basis.

So where is the UK's thinking now? While clearly wanting an economically strong eurozone with which to trade given its importance for our economy, we are also encouraging a fiscal union even though that would ultimately imply a political union that would exclude us. Similarly, we are encouraging the development of a banking union to ensure that banks are properly supervised, capitalised and supported, again an important plank of a strong economy, but without having seriously thought about what the implications might be for the UK and the City of London in particular.

But perhaps there are some lessons that the UK can teach the world in relation to crisis management. There is amazement, among UK politicians, commentators and businesses, at the inability of the politicians in the eurozone to get their act together and to realise that decisions need to be taken quickly, as the UK did at the beginning of the crisis. If decisions are not taken quickly, the markets take over and one's grip over the situation disappears – a bit like what we are observing in Europe right now. Alistair Darling recalls the actions as soon as the financial crisis started in 2007 when he was Chancellor. The reason why what the government did then to control the situation worked was 'because people were taken aback at the scale of what we did and the speed at which we did it'. He believes that 'if you have a problem like this, firstly you can't delay and your response has to be more substantial than people expect, and it has to be quicker than people expect'. The other critical element of it is quickly getting international support, and he recalls how, within a few days, the government was able to persuade the Americans subtly to change their own policy towards their financial sector to be more in line with the UK approach. It was also important to get positive responses from the other European countries. He points out how Sarkozy, for example, got Gordon Brown to attend the meeting of the eurozone leaders, which, explains Darling, 'is something Britain had never gone to before, and was really quite a big landmark'.

The point was that in the space of less than a week you had the drama of RBS collapsing, which it effectively did, and you had the announcement of the rescue package, and then you had the other countries coming in line. It didn't resolve the problem but it stabilised it, and stopped the fire from spreading.

But others did not move as fast as we did and that has been a fundamental problem with Europe – while its rhetoric was fine, which actually helped stabilise markets for a while, the deeper problems were not dealt with. The Irish banking crisis situation, and now Spain and others, are a good example of this, and UK policy makers and politicians have a good reason to argue that because the UK took the action it did early on UK banks are in a much better position than those in many countries in Europe. Ireland underwrote its banks and sowed the seeds of its downfall two years later when it eventually had to go to the IMF and the eurozone to get bailed out. The UK uniquely stepped in and helped Ireland directly with £7bn funding as part of the November Irish bail-out, which injected a total of €85bn into the Irish economy, of which €70bn went into the banking sector. The UK also extended bilateral loans to stabilise the Irish banking system, as it is clearly in Britain's national interest that the economy is successful and it has a stable banking system. Alistair Darling says that he had to endure lectures from his Spanish opposite number on how good the Spanish regulatory system was and how they had no problems with their banks. If you look at Germany, too, you do wonder what *Landesbanken* were doing buying subprime mortgages in Florida when these banks were set up to service the German economy. And banks in other countries are also now coming under the spotlight. This helps explain where various countries were coming from in the Greek negotiations. When the then French Finance Minister Christine Lagarde took the lead in wanting to do something about Greece, it is quite possible that this wasn't simply based on empathy towards Greece but rather a result of the French banks being quite exposed to the Greek banks. It has in fact been suggested that the first Greek bail-out, which was negotiated just before the coalition government took over, was very much to France's advantage. The implications for the French banking system if Greece had been let go would have been enormous. Understanding this should help shape the UK's position on the eurozone crisis and guide the coalition's attempts to influence the course of events in Europe rather than head for the exit.

The reason for caution and the need for constructive engagement by the UK is that this isn't only a specific Greek problem. Instead there is a parallel – even bigger – issue that needs to be addressed: money from other countries financed the booms and asset bubbles in the periphery. A lot of German and other European money went into Spain and Ireland in the property booms there and it is worth noting that when the crisis first hit, the Irish government in taking its actions was particularly mindful of the impact that defaulting Irish banks might have on European institutions.

WHAT NEXT?

A real problem with the eurozone governance process is that the conclusion of each summit is often too little, too late. The markets perk up for a few days but the honeymoon period is getting shorter and shorter. It used to last a couple of months. This became a couple of weeks, then a few hours, and now it is at times reduced to twenty minutes! What is clear is that the biggest European problem is the underperformance of its banking system. The regulators allowed themselves to be persuaded that if people were making money and the economies were growing, it was probably OK. And when problems hit individual countries, they completely failed to take on board the interconnections between banks across countries. It is clear that you can't assess one individual bank and stress-test it by just focusing on national scenarios, without asking yourself what would happen if your next-door neighbour collapsed. And that is where the regulatory system went wrong. Banks were trading with a lot less capital than in the past. People assumed they could always get access to funds so they weren't particularly obsessed with liquidity issues, which obviously become acute in times of crisis. Alistair Darling used the following analogy about the problem of regulators in this interconnected financial world:

You go into a house and you can smell rot some-where. You lift the carpet and you can't see anything. Then you put down the carpet and you say well, that's alright. But the smell is still there. You have to pull the floorboards up. And finally you have to rip the whole house apart and start again because the rot is still there and it will keep causing damage. We can see how there was something rotten in the way economies were run and we have not really owned up to that failure.

The European institutions and politicians didn't 'get it'. When the crisis first hit, however, the UK dealt with the issue earlier. It now has a crucial role to play in assisting the rest of the eurozone to respond just as sensibly.

10

WHAT NEXT FOR GREECE?

So what next for Greece? It is difficult to tell as the patient appears terminally ill. Some people speak of hidden opportunities. Nobody speaks of hope. And without hope the country will go under. And the fear is that it will then drag the whole euro project down with it. It is this that European leaders have still not understood.

It is not only the European political class. Some well-known economists take the same stance. Meghnad Desai, who may have just managed to avoid teaching me at the LSE, believes that a Greek exit may be Europe's chance, referring to 'Grexit' as 'a weird creature from Dr Seuss, the fabled children's storyteller'. But I am grateful to him for highlighting a poem written by Günter Grass, the German Nobel Prize winner who, unlike most Germans, writes of Europe's shame in its abandonment of Greece, calling it a 'land that lost its rights' and warning that without its spirit 'Europe will be soulless'.

I couldn't agree more. The truth is that Greece is

not the cause of the eurozone crisis. It is instead the symptom of a system that was never designed to cope with situations of the sort we are going through and which has hit countries like Greece disproportionately.

We therefore need to look at Greece as it is now and its ability to pull itself out of its current despair. Critically, this is going to depend on its neighbours and European partners. Greece cannot pull itself out of this on its own. Even if it were to leave the euro, default on its debts, maybe even leave the EU entirely – as the unreformed Communist Party would have Greece do – the country would collapse into depression, possibly accompanied by hyperinflation. So the question is, how can Greece and the rest of Europe devise – and deliver – a solution that restores hope of prosperity to Greece, preserves democracy and contributes to securing the future of the eurozone as a whole?

THE MAN WHO WOULD BE KING

The responsibility for pulling Greece out of the current mess now falls to a new coalition government headed by Antonis Samaras, the leader of New Democracy, the conservative party that narrowly won Greece's 17 June 2012 elections. Samaras was so eager to fulfil his life-long ambition to become Prime Minister that he went ahead and took the oath of office days before he appointed his Cabinet following lengthy negotiations with his coalition partners, socialist Pasok and leftist DIMAR (DIMAR would leave the coalition a year later). It is an open secret that Antonis Samaras has worked all his life to become Prime Minister of Greece but everyone is already asking if the coalition he has put together will last.

Martin Schulz, the President of the European Parliament, captured the early wariness towards the new Greek Prime Minister. 'Mr Samaras has not made himself known for his reliable comments,' Mr Schulz told German public television. 'In the past, he was one of those who rejected all reform measures proposed by George Papandreou.' In the process, Samaras dropped twenty-one MPs from his party who voted for the first bail-out package, and saw two splinter parties formed as a result. One, the right-wing Independent Greeks, won 11% in the 6 May 2012 elections and 6% in the 17 June elections. The other, led by Dora Bakoyannis, who had stood against him in 2009 for the New Democracy leadership, tanked in the first elections but rejoined New Democracy for the second. In the interim, Samaras had changed his tune from being against the bail-out to being a proponent of the second bail-out, though wanting to renegotiate some of its terms.

Yet, despite doubts, Samaras confirmed in writing to the leaders of the European Council of 28–29 June 2012 that his government 'owned the responsibility' of seeing through the bail-out agreements, albeit with a request for more time to achieve adherence and some corrections in the terms, in order to slow the downward spiral of the Greek economy.

Samaras's Cabinet is loaded with New Democracy MPs who stuck with their leader. His coalition partners,

Pasok and DIMAR, chose to nominate unelected party officials rather than elected MPs, which could be interpreted as a sign of wanting to place a little political distance between their leaders and the undoubtedly unpopular decisions that the Cabinet will be asked to take. Twenty-six of the thirty-nine Cabinet members in the seventeen ministries called upon to put Greece back on track have never been part of a Cabinet before. Most are elected politicians, party operatives or professors – not obviously a Cabinet equipped with much technical expertise for the job ahead. The only two nominated with related experience were the Minister of Finance, Vassilis Rapanos, who was the President of the National Bank of Greece, and the Deputy Minister of Seas and Shipping, George Vernicos, a successful ship owner. Unfortunately, they both resigned – Vernicos because he owned offshore shipping companies and Rapanos on health grounds, even before he visited his new office. Samaras himself underwent an eye operation a couple of days after the elections, something that kept him from attending the EU summit of 28–29 June as well as the Euro 2012 quarter-final against Germany! Evidently the task of tackling Greece's financial problems is not good for one's health!

A month later the government announced the names of the fifty-two General Secretary positions in the seventeen ministries. The General Secretary is another Greek bureaucratic creation of political significance, effectively running a ministry by following the relevant minister's policy direction. In most countries, this is a permanent position held by a technocrat to ensure continuity and enable politicians to implement their policies. In Greece, it is a political position which is filled by the minister's choice. Thirty-two were selected by New Democracy, fourteen by Pasok and six by DIMAR. Many were politicians looking for jobs after failing to be elected during the 2012 elections.

So once again Greece got a political administration rather than a technocrat one. The new government had to make difficult decisions and shoulder the responsibility for – and implement – previous equally difficult decisions. Political legitimacy at these times is important. But although the coalition enjoyed a shortlived handsome parliamentary majority, only about half of those who voted cast their vote for one of the three parties in the government. The worry was that, in addition to a narrow and fragile political base, the new government might have, in a new and worrying way, combined (relative) inexperience with the bad habits of its predecessors.

In this area everyone looked at political appointments and other signs of change or otherwise. Soon after forming his government in the summer of 2012, Samaras replaced the Head of the Financial Police (SDOE), a well-known prosecuting attorney who exposed deceit and tax evasion among major Greek and multinational companies during his tenure, with the Head of the Tax Office of the rural state of Messinia, located in the Peloponnese, where Samaras was elected. This was part of sweeping changes among ten key government directorates and secretariats, with New Democracy reappointing six, Pasok two and DIMAR two. Internal and external commentators and observers wondered whether the motive for the changes was increased efficiency or rather an attempt to guarantee party influence over significant areas of the Greek public sector.

So one year on, where is Greece now? Still not out of the woods, by a long way. The instability of Greek politics was highlighted again in the summer of 2013 by the decision to close down Greece's equivalent of the BBC, the public service broadcaster ERT, firing some 2,650 employees in the process. The decision received large-scale protests and was partly reversed. It will reopen under a slightly different name – NERIT – and hire back many of its former employees but at much lower salaries. But the episode showed how rattled and shaky Greek politics remains.

Nevertheless, in some ways things are not as bad as they seem despite the fact that the coalition now has only a majority of three in Parliament. Although the ERT closure was cause enough for DIMAR to withdraw from the coalition, the fact is that by then their popularity had dropped from 7% to 4% in the polls. In fact, it looks like both Samaras and Evangelos Venizelos, the leader of Pasok, had played it smart. Venizelos in particular managed to remain in the governing coalition even though the party he finally managed to take over had slid from 12% of the votes in 2012's elections to below 6% in the polls a year later. The Papandreou name that had shadowed his ambitions for decades had disappeared from view. Other party barons had been jailed or were criminally investigated. Others – now effectively unemployed and unemployable – had formed fringe political parties in the hope they would garner enough votes to receive state funds in the future. The Samaras–Venizelos deal elevated the latter to Vice President and Minister of Foreign Affairs, giving him increased exposure in Greece and among Greece's interlocutors abroad. And Venizelos cleverly pointed the finger at former Minister of Finance, George Papaconstantinou, as the culprit who removed the names of his three relatives from the infamous Lagarde List containing the names of tax evaders with secret bank accounts at one Swiss bank branch of HSBC where €2bn of Greek money was parked. In the process he managed to stave off accusations of mishandling the list he himself had inherited from Papaconstandinou in a 2011 government reshuffle, which he kept in his drawer for a year and a half, even at a time when he was not in government.

Samaras, helped by his able Finance Minister Stournaras, has generally had a good press and despite the current fragility in the political process (including the detention in September 2013 of party leaders of the neo-Nazi Golden Dawn party) seems to be holding on. Meanwhile, Syriza, which held its congress in late spring, has transformed itself from an agglomeration of radical leftist movements into a proper political party under its young leader Tsipras, achieving some

30% of the votes, although it still attracts a significant measure of internal discontent. Its political voice, however, has been notably weaker. Samaras and Venizelos, both of whom at various stages in the past had objected to the troika dictat, are now the ones Greece's political allies and creditors must rely upon to get their agenda through. It is a very interesting turn of events involving the two parties that have dominated Greek politics for the past forty years and whose policies brought the nation into receivership. But it may be what politics is all about: 'flow with the blow'! Ancient Greek historian Thoukidides describes the political scene in democratic Athens 2,500 years ago: 'Noble, intelligent men with noble ideas proclaiming public benefit, quickly change their agendas to personal benefit, thus inflicting devastating pain to those who voted them in.'

WHAT ARE THE HOPES FOR RECOVERY?

Are there real prospects for Greece to get out of this crisis? Will Greece decide it has had enough? Will Greece recover before the world abandons it out of fatigue and out of the realisation that there are bigger problems out there, like Spain and Italy?

One school of thought hopes the country will ride it out on auto-pilot, following the troika's guidelines. But what is being mandated by the troika has never been successfully applied in such magnitude. Nobody knows if the measures devised by it, aimed uniquely at limiting creditor damage and contagion, will work.

The political system still seems ill-equipped for delivering substantial and painful change. Up until now, the parties vying for votes did not dare to support measures that were damaging to specific interest groups. They counted the swing votes from specific voting segments of the population affected by measures they oppose, with the unions providing the key votes. The result had been resistance to firing in the public sector, to closures, consolidations or privatisations of state companies or any real liberalisation of protectionist closed professions (trucking, taxis, pharmacists, lawyers and notaries among others) for fear of losing their votes. Instead, the parties opted for repeated horizontal measures that affected all Greeks, such as higher VAT, lower tax deductibles, lower base salaries and pensions etc. while blaming the troika for their imposition. This trend seems to be continuing even now though it is no longer sustainable. It is true that on the eve of the troika's demands for additional measures to shave another €11.5bn off state expenses, Samaras did announce a 30% reduction in the cost of government by rationalising its operations and closing down or merging state agencies and enterprises. But, in the same breath, he publicly reassured the nation that the 30% cut in the government's operating budget would be achieved without a single firing!

In summer 2012, the new Finance Minister, Yannis Stournaras, Greece's delegate and chief negotiator with the troika, summoned all the ministers in the government to hear their proposals for cuts to help meet this

30% target. It was no surprise that the cuts conceded by each ministry were apparently tiny and the total they offered was totally inadequate. The new Justice Minister refused to reduce the salaries and benefits of judges and the new Defence Minister refused to reduce the salaries and benefits of uniformed personnel. The Minister of Administration, responsible for streamlining government operations, was also not forthcoming with cost reductions in his own ministry.

Some progress has been made, for example, the abolishing of the absurdities of the regulations and privileges surrounding the so called 'hardship professions'. However, the task of the new government in securing further cuts might become harder rather than easier. The limited scope for further across-the-board cuts in benefits or increases in taxation is now recognised – including by the troika team itself. The focus will increasingly be on targeted measures. There are plenty of anomalies and distortions in Greece crying out for remedial action – but a similarly long list of interest groups will be lining up to defend them.

Public sector reforms, in particular reducing the number of public servants, are now the focus of troika attention. It looks like Prime Minister Samaras and his Finance Minister Stournaras are becoming serious about delivering those cuts as a condition for the latest troika bail-out dispersal in July 2013. But it is easier said than done. Moving a public servant in Greece from a redundant position to a productive reassignment seems to take a minimum of twelve months to be effected. To give two examples, first consider the school on the remote island of St. Eustache (Aghios Efstratios) which has eighteen students and employs twenty-nine educators, seventeen of which are gym teachers! The teachers' whereabouts remain unknown. Second, take the Athens journalist Yannis Palaiologos who highlighted in *Time* Athens' municipally owned radio station which had an annual revenue of €300,000 but cost the taxpayer more €13m to run. A new manager appointed by Athens' reforming mayor, George Kaminis, to run the station declared: 'We couldn't keep overpaying for people who had three or four other jobs, at a time of mass unemployment among journalists.' These examples of public payroll padding are now becoming known. But the issue is difficult to tackle effectively as no one gives up a job and income easily and without growth and new jobs to go to the misery of the labour market has added to social tension – and this has been exploited by extremist rhetoric from the left as well as the dangerously neo-Nazi members of the Golden Dawn party.

The closure of the public broadcaster, ERT, was a good example of an attempt to meet the troika's quota of public sector staff reductions. ERT was an easy target because it is incorporated as a private entity whose sole shareholder is the state. The public service bureaucracy was, thus, bypassed. More state-controlled companies unsuitable for privatisation may face similar shocks in the near future. The ERT closure was cause enough for DIMAR to withdraw from the coalition. Though the closure was reversed, the shock effect led to an acceptance that a smaller payroll could continue to sustain public service broadcasting.

The sale of state holdings forms an important part of the deficit reduction programme. It was estimated that the assets singled out for disposal would bring in €50bn. A special vehicle called the Hellenic Republic Assets Development Fund (HRADF) was set up to manage the portfolio of state assets and their sale. It took a long time for the process to get going and for a while not much happened. Though advisors were hired, the legislative process required to enable the sale of the assets was exceedingly slow. The result was that after the sale of a stake of the telecoms company OTE to Deutsche Telekom in 2011, there was no revenue from any privatisations in 2012 and sales targets have been thrown out the window. Foreign interest is slow to materialise due to the instability in Greece and the bad publicity it gets. It is true that the expectations of what Greece could receive from the sale of state assets had probably been widely exaggerated, particularly given the dire economic situation in the country. But two years have still been lost!

Indeed, following the failure at the last moment to sell DEPA, the state natural gas company, to Gazprom, the commission has since substantially reduced the target for sale of public assets for 2013. Total cumulative proceeds by 2020 are now not expected to exceed €25bn. What is more, there have been frequent changes to the chair of HRADF, responsible for getting the privatisation process going, which either reflects the government of the time or just the latest series of scandals – the most recent chair of the organisation resigned in August 2013, just six months after his predecessor, for accepting a trip in the private plane owned by the person whose consortium had just bid successfully for OPAP, the hugely treasured state lottery company. With process so slow the European Commission proposed in mid-2013 the idea of moving the real estate assets under HRADF to a Greek-owned but Luxembourg-based holding company which they believed would be able to expedite the whole process. In early September 2013, the Greeks indicated strongly that they would not agree to the solution, which they fear would lose them control of the process. Progress will remain slow for the foreseeable future.

There are clear signs of fatigue by all concerned, but mostly by the Greek people. One month after it was formed, the new government's cumulative (three-party) approval rating trailed the people's first choice in the elections: 'none of the above'. Yet there was still some hope. The Bank of Greece reported that €10bn made it back to Greek banks in the three weeks after the new government was formed. More money has returned since, but slowly, and the four main banks have seen their deposits shrink by a third since 2009.

The lack of liquidity has reached new heights. As part of the recapitalisation process of the Greek banks, which speeded up what was already happening anyway, some dozen smaller banks were wound down or withdrew from what was a very difficult market and some of their assets were taken over by the bigger banks which now controlled around 90% of the Greek market. But the situation remains a very fragile one. The banks themselves were hit by a later 'haircut' in 2012 and the subsequent private sector involvement (PSI) in their holdings of Greek sovereign debt. They still have to deal with increasingly bad losses on their lending. Non-performing loans were estimated in mid-2013 to run at around 30% for the banking sector as a whole. As wages dropped significantly and unemployment rocketed, consumer credit has been declining year after year since the crisis started. And, purportedly for the protection of the public interest, the banks have also been directed to hold – in cash deposits or collateral – the amounts of consumer credit accorded to individuals and businesses. As a result, banks who have issued credit cards are summarily cancelling the ones on which nothing is owed, while reducing the credit limit of others to the amount owed on the last statement. In some cases they are being replaced by debit cards. Collateral has vanished because of the drop in real-estate values, while factoring is no longer a viable borrowing instrument, as the payment of invoices becomes doubtful. Greece is turning into a cash economy. People are selling their valuables and their assets in fire sales to meet subsistence needs or turning to loan sharks for temporary relief.

The availability of credit for businesses, particularly

SMEs, remains dire. It is true that lending is dropping across most countries in Europe as economies have shrunk and banks are trying to rebuild their capital base. But for many periphery countries, and in particular Greece, the poor creditworthiness of the banks themselves is starving businesses of much-needed credit to enable them to sell abroad – which is the only growth avenue there might be for many. The result is that businesses in Greece are starved of cash. This has prompted the Germans to suggest starting an offshoot of their own specialist SME bank, KFW, with an initial fund of €100m supplemented by money coming from the Greek banks to provide extra urgent help to those companies.

That may help. But it is all happening too slowly. Since 2010, rents in the commercial centre of Athens have dropped by 50%. But so has occupancy. Some 42% of the retail space on Stadiou Street, the 'Oxford Street' in the centre of Athens, is currently unoccupied. On fashionable Tsakalov Street in Kolonaki, 34% of the shops lie empty. If it isn't for the economic crisis, it is because these streets suffer the wrath of anarchists who partake in the frequent demonstrations that create havoc in downtown Athens and dissuade shoppers from venturing there. As a result, the desecration of the city centre has turned this once-thriving area of Athens into a ghetto.

A TIME FOR GENEROSITY

Many commentators – and the markets – still see a significant risk of Greece leaving the euro in the near future. The new government had a sizeable enough majority to cope with the odd protest vote and defection. But its long-term viability is still in question following DIMAR's exit from the coalition in mid-2013. Samaras did obtain some lengthening of the repayment schedule but the language from German ministers, at least prior to the federal elections in September 2012, has remained intransigent.

Everyone knows that Greece's current position is unsustainable. The debts will not be repaid even if the country is brought to its knees by continued austerity and there will be no popular acquiescence to further hardship if there is no light at the end of the tunnel. There will be some movement but the question is how much. As expected the minimal outcome was some rescheduling of repayment – with Greece being given extra time to reduce its deficit and with some modest (implicit) write-off of its debts. But it is unlikely to be enough.

Despite progress, many areas need further attention – health costs are still too high in relation to GDP and there are abuses of the system. There have been moves to online prescriptions for medicines to reduce abuses and bring costs under control, but more can be done. Electronic procurement across the public sector and better coordination would make a big difference here. Professions need to be opened up further. The taxation system needs complete overhaul and the tax base needs to be extended to bring in areas of the society that pay very little, like the Greek Orthodox Church. More cuts need to be made in the bureaucracy and administration and in public spending but in an acceptable way, not just by penalising the elderly through further pension cuts and, to borrow a phrase from British politics, by continuously 'squeezing the hardworking middle'.

Fairness will be important here. The tax system needs to become more stable to enable investment, which is so essential to growth. The Greek government has now created an agency to organise and supervise the collection of taxes, headed by a young technocrat who was until recently working at a university in London. In the first half of 2013, there were 1,433 arrests for tax evasion, representing €8.5bn in past due taxes, and some offenders were given jail sentences. But that was just the first harvest of the year. By the end of July 2013, what remained uncollected amounted to a staggering €60bn. To some extent this can be explained by the fact that both individuals and businesses are strapped for cash and because the change in the administration of the tax system has caused delays in tax collections. But the figure is still enormous. In addition, avoiding the tax system altogether is a favourite Greek pastime, with tax evasion particularly prevalent among small businesses. From 6 to 8 August 2013, the Financial Police went on 'holiday' to the Greek islands. They checked 586 enterprises, mostly in the food, beverage and entertainment business, and found that 5,668 infractions had been committed. Statistically, 100% of those checked in the islands of Paxoi, Symi and Amorgos committed infractions, mostly on rendering VAT; 96% in Santorini; 81% in Rhodes; 80% in

Mykonos and Andros; 78% in Paros; 63% in Crete; and 54% in the Athens Metropolitan area. In desperation the Greek government has forced every shop to post a sign stating the new law. The law stipulates that a customer presented with a bill not coming from a cash register, in other words without an accompanying proof of purchase, has the right to leave the establishment without paying it. Enforcing the law is easier said than done. On a recent visit I noticed an incident that was reported of young customers walking out of a bar when no receipt was forthcoming, only to be chased by the bouncers and beaten badly for allegedly trying to run away without paying their bill.

But keen to collect taxes and meet bail-out conditions, the government is hitting all the easy targets – and many times over. There have been sixteen different new tax measures affecting personal property. Figuring out how to calculate them is only secondary to people's ability to pay them. The 'have-nots' point at the 'haves', who still seem to enjoy tax breaks.

Greeks know the system is corrupt and help sustain it. Paying a fine, if ever caught, is cheaper than abiding by the laws. The legal system is so inefficient that there is little danger of punishment. On the eve of the next election, whenever that might be, they know that the winning party will forgive or 'settle' their issues. The costs to the economy of this disruptive behaviour is disregarded by the politicians. The political gain from accommodating them is more valuable to the system. Nevertheless, pushed by the troika and by the need to institute a rational tax environment to encourage and reward proper market behaviour, a number of ideas were recently floated by the Ministry of Finance, to be voted in before the end of 2013, aimed at encouraging citizens to behave in a way that prevents these types of tax evasion by businesses. They include a deduction from personal taxable income of up to double the face value of receipt-VAT burdened expenses from doctors, lawyers, plumbers, electricians, car mechanics and all those professionals considered as perennial tax evaders. In addition, in order to increase visibility of the sales taking place and hence ensure the collection of VAT due, the government is proposing a personal tax rebate related to the annual value of debit and credit card payments to discourage cash purchases. Similarly, with a country full of people who love eating out staying at home, VAT on meals out was cut from 23% to 13% from 1 August 2013. There is little point raising VAT if no one is spending any money.

It is perfectly understandable why all this is going on. In the first seven months of 2013, the government actually achieved a primary surplus of €2.6bn when it was expected to be in deficit by some €3.1bn. The IMF, including Christine Lagarde in an interview in the summer of 2013, praised the Greek government's efforts. But this improvement was due mainly to lower public sector investment, structural funds coming in from the EU that swelled the Ministry of Finance's coffers and also repayments by eurozone central banks of profits they had made on Greek sovereign bonds. It did not represent a fundamental change in the Greek economy. Actual tax receipts were in fact way below target levels, partly because of the inability so far to properly tap the Greek tax base. In reality tax revenues were low mostly because of a continually shrinking economy where everyone has been cutting back, where fewer and fewer people are employed and where companies are going out of business. Indeed, some 90,000 enterprises are estimated to close their doors in 2013, adding 150,000 people to the unemployment ranks. The Greek middle class, which took thirty years to become established, is being eradicated at an alarming pace. In this environment tax receipts are bound to suffer and fiscal consolidation becomes harder to achieve.

The fall in GDP in the second quarter of 2013 marks the twentieth consecutive quarter of economic decline, leaving the country in an economic hole that some have termed a depression. Growth forecasts detailing an improvement in economic activity have been postponed yet again, this time possibly until 2014. It will take years before the economy reaches pre-crisis levels again; it has shrunk by roughly 24% since 2009. The policy of spending cuts and tax increases demanded by creditors to cure public finances has reduced the deficit but savaged the economy and society.

The statistics bear some resemblance to those during the Great Depression in the US, when gross domestic product fell 27% during 1929–1933, while unemployment climbed to more than 20%. Although there is no fixed definition of depression, economist Barry Bosworth at the Brookings Institution says Greece qualifies as experiencing it because of the unusual depth and length of its downturn. 'It goes way beyond anything that looks like a recession,' he said. 'It's absolutely appropriate to refer to Greece as in a depression.'

At the same time, although the uncertainty about Greece staying in the eurozone is ebbing away, the damage it has done to confidence in the country may be irreversible. There are countless examples of money either flowing out of the country or money pledged being frozen. The €5bn deal signed with the Qataris a couple of years ago to invest in the old airport complex and turn it into a major international business centre foundered because of uncertainty about the future and has necessitated a new competition for the right to develop a site largely unused since the Athens Olympics eight years ago. There are many in the last and current government who are concerned that all this Greek-bashing has not helped confidence. The Greeks are blamed for their prevarication and uncouth negotiating tactics, but it is also difficult to negotiate with the troika while keeping voters happy and informed. I suspect the IMF is the easiest party to negotiate with given its structure but dealing with the European Commission and the ECB actually means having to deal with sixteen (and since July 2013, seventeen) other countries all with different perspectives – look at the Finns, for example, who insisted on collateral from Greece as part of the bail-out conditions. And remember that the IMF, so blamed by the Greeks for its tough stance, possibly unfairly, was dealing with a problem different in scale to any it had attempted to resolve before. The largest deal they had arranged before Greece was the $30bn rescue of Brazil. The two Greek rescues were much larger at €240bn and also required a different type of approach than the usual one meted out to developing countries. That is why the comparisons some make with Argentina or Malaysia are fatuous. Argentina, unlike Greece, is a major commodity producer that benefited from devaluation. But today it remains relatively poor with considerable political and social tensions. Malaysia can impose solutions on its people that a mature European democracy cannot. Greeks do not want a return to 1967 nor to revert to the poverty of a drachma economy in order to please economic theoreticians who do not live in the country.

In essence, the time frame for Greek reform was too short, technical assistance came late and the austerity measures were too harsh and did not take into account the impact they would have on the economy and the inability of the Greek system to reform in a hurry. They were the wrong recipes at the wrong time, not just for Greece but also for most of the periphery countries.

The IMF, in its mid-2013 Fourth Evaluation Report, said that Greece had made 'important progress in rectifying pre-crisis imbalances' and that the economy was 'rebalancing'. Nice terminology. But the fund itself noted that 'the gains had come as a result of recession which has suppressed imports', and not through 'productivity-enhancing structural reform'. No one doubts that significant further restructuring would be needed to achieve what the troika calls a sustainability target: a debt-to-GDP ratio of 120% by 2020, currently at 175% and rising.

I have been arguing for some time that Greece needs to be treated more generously. As mentioned before and as people now increasingly acknowledge, Germany has benefited greatly over the last decade from the creation of the eurozone. We are now reaching the point where some of those benefits have to be paid for. The costs to Germany of Greece leaving the eurozone will be substantial because of the financial contagion. The costs of continued uncertainty – in terms of lower growth – are significant. The lowest-cost solution all round is likely to be a deal where there is a further substantial write-off of Greek debt combined with meaningful EU investment in Greece's productive capacity through the structural funds, but where, in return, Greece makes a genuine and verifiable commitment to continued administrative and structural reform. The solution would in my view require as the next step a further 'haircut', so far resisted, that would apply to public holders of debt in a similar way as the one of February 2012 applied to private holders of Greek debt.

Might we term this a new Marshall (or Merkel?) Plan for Greece? I think the Greek population might see this as a long-overdue recognition by the rest of Europe of Greece's geopolitical significance, of the pain it has already had to bear and of the fact that though far from blameless its current position is not entirely due to the actions of the Greeks or their governments. But this would require a change in the attitude of Germany and other 'core' eurozone members, which in turn requires the politicians there to provide a fuller and rather more nuanced explanation of the challenges – and responsibilities – of living in a monetary union. The therapy employed to cure Greece hasn't worked and will not work for as long as the focus lies on securing loan repayments. Like dealing with a naughty child, spoiled by its elders, punishment alone is not the recommended remedy. Coaching and encouragement work better. Write off the broken china and show the children how to set the table properly. Then join them for dinner.

11

WHAT NEXT FOR THE EURO? CAN IT BE SAVED – AND SHOULD IT BE SAVED?

Latterly the story of the euro has been one crisis after another. Greece, Ireland and Portugal were in turn forced to seek bail-outs (in the case of Greece, two bail-outs). Spain has been forced to accept European financial support for its banking sector, while being insistent it is not a full-scale bail-out and hence not requiring the same degree of surveillance and interference in its domestic policies. Cyprus has become the next casualty because of its exposure to Greece. But nobody thinks we are out of the woods yet. Italy has been the latest country to become the focus of attention and intense market pressure and the markets expect both Spain and Italy to ask for full bail-outs at some stage.

The founders of the European idea, Monnet and Schuman, believed that Europe would forge ever closer union through a series of crises. We are going through one protracted crisis now and, perhaps, the severity of the crisis has forced an acceleration in the pace of integration. But it has also shown the limits of our political institutions and that in a globalised environment they are always one step behind the markets, if not several steps. They are forced to react to issues which, by the time a possible solution has been found, have already been overtaken by events requiring further, even more drastic, intervention to which the political system cannot respond fast enough or satisfactorily enough to calm things down. And the cost to the European economies, to the social cohesion across Europe and to political and economic freedom is immense. It is no wonder that a greater – and wider – range of voices is questioning whether the euro can, or indeed should, survive.

It is clear now that the blueprint for European Monetary Union (EMU) agreed at Maastricht was flawed in a number of respects. Most obviously, as discussed in Chapter 2, the bloc of eurozone candidate countries failed the test of an optimal currency area. Their economies had not converged and did not converge. Maybe Germany, Austria and the Benelux economies were close enough to make a success of a single currency but the peripheral economies of Spain, Italy, Greece and Portugal (and Ireland for that matter) patently were not. In that environment, monetary union makes little sense. Since the creation of the euro, the single European Central Bank (ECB) interest rate has mostly been too high for Germany and too low for many of the periphery countries. This has encouraged a spending spree in the periphery countries by both the private sector – households and firms – and the public sector, which saw its sovereign borrowing costs drop markedly as interest rates converged. This was further encouraged by the lifting of the balance of payments and exchange rate constraints as different currencies disappeared, giving way to the euro. Capital flows to the periphery countries increased markedly as there was no currency risk attached – further destabilising these countries. Money was plentiful and high rewards were chased, however risky. As a result, even during the 'good' years, eurozone membership exacerbated the effects of the asymmetric shocks hitting the various economies. The easy availability of credit created great expansion in borrowing and in places like Spain and Ireland this led to a huge property boom which caused serious problems to the banking system when the bubble burst. In fact, in the good years the pressure to embark on much-needed structural reform by the periphery countries, the PIIGS (Portugal, Ireland, Italy, Greece and Spain), was reduced as the economies seemed, on the surface at least, to be doing well, in most cases growing strongly with rapidly rising incomes. The euro was seen to be a good thing and attention moved away from any fundamental flaws. This meant these economies were in a much more precarious position than they might have been when the financial crisis broke in 2008.

But economic considerations did not seem to matter to political élites across continental Europe, who were wedded to the concept of the euro – and not just the usual Europhile suspects (Germany, France, Italy, Benelux). Politicians in Greece, Portugal and Spain had seen EU membership as a means of cementing fledgling democracies. They were reluctant to skip the chance of membership of the eurozone when it came along, even if some of them did have to be creative with the statistics and even though the economics suggested that membership would be a mistake. Indeed, there was a feeling that euro membership would somehow enable their economies to modernise and catch up with the better-performing northern ones – as if by magic.

The Maastricht blueprint failed to put in place the other necessary conditions to make the euro succeed. There was no lender of last resort. There were insufficient fiscal transfers between rich and poor parts of the eurozone. And the measures designed to ensure fiscal discipline and improve the competitiveness of the lagging countries were insufficient and then watered down as soon as they became a nuisance to France and Germany.

Twenty years on, the consequences of this flawed master plan are apparent. The eurozone problems are now having an impact across the world. Even China's economy is feeling the pinch, with export growth slowing due to weak conditions in European markets. EU leaders working with the IMF sought first to stabilise the situation and rescue those economies that had hit the rocks. Increasingly it has become obvious that calming the markets and saving the single currency is about more than bail-outs, injections of liquidity and fiscal consolidation. It requires deep-seated reforms to the governance of the eurozone and, almost inevitably, changes to the character of the entire EU. We have already seen evidence of this in the decision of twenty-five of the twenty-seven EU member states to sign a new intergovernmental treaty setting in place the fiscal compact. With the ink barely dry on the original signatures, and indeed the Treaty still to be formally ratified and put in place, further steps towards integration are underway. But will they be enough to stabilise the situation? Will they satisfy Europe's voters? And are they economically or politically sensible and desirable?

WHAT NEEDS TO BE DONE?

So the euro was misconceived and, even worse, it was very badly applied because its founders did not know what they were dealing with. The idea that an exchange rate union alone would encourage prudent behaviour and convergence was laughable. The countries had very different cultures, were in different stages of development and had different institutional structures. There were different levels of decentralisation (in some cases regional autonomy was strong and with it regional bureaucracy) and the role taken by the state in economic life varied. And the differences do not end there. Look at the varying sizes of their underground economies, the pressure from migration, the gap in incomes. The euro made those differences even larger. The principle of a 'social contract' between the state and its people that has existed in various countries for decades if not centuries cannot be unwound without protest and resistance overnight, and Greece is a very good example of this. Indeed, over the past couple of years most governments in Europe that have introduced austerity programmes have lost power in elections.

In reality, the root of the eurozone's problem is one of competitiveness, not fiscal indiscipline – although fiscal indiscipline is undesirable and makes the problem worse. The peripheral economies have, in general, significantly lower productivity per head than Germany or other leading economies. And the removal of exchange rate risk meant that no one worried about the balance of payments, which used to be a major constraint in the past. If you spent a lot abroad in the old days and weren't receiving enough foreign exchange in return this tended to act as an 'automatic stabiliser' of sorts. The currency would drop, making imports more expensive and exports cheaper, and any rise in interest rates needed to limit pressure on the currency would choke off demand. Imports would then fall as demand shifted to comparatively cheaper domestically produced goods. That would have been a classic response until recently. With the elimination of this constraint, the incentive to focus on one's own domestic productive capacity disappeared and there was a huge transfer of funds from the periphery countries to northern Europe, particularly to Germany, whose products the Greeks and others bought with abandon. Germany saw large surpluses emerge in its trade with the rest of

Europe, but no one focused on the increasing deficits of the countries buying German goods. And the financial markets were blinded because they thought no country could possibly be allowed to default. They continued to lend cheaply, equating Greek and Spanish risk to that of Germany. Inevitably both the bank and sovereign downgrades that we have seen led to a huge correction of all this in only a couple of years.

So how does one deal with the issue of competitiveness? It is less of a problem if wages can fall to make up for lower productivity or if the currency is able to devalue to accommodate nominal wage increases. But neither has happened.

First, nominal wages are very sticky downwards – in other words, although they tend to rise in response to higher inflation, it is always difficult to cut them in hard times as there is a lot of resistance from the workers to see nominal falls in living standards. Instead, periphery/low-cost countries were seeing their wages rise faster to catch up with each other than the much more advanced mature economies. This had been widely expected and indeed was one of the ways the benefits of the single market were meant to come through to those countries – they were, after all, starting from a lower base and further integration would boost demand for their (cheaper) products and services once exchange risk was removed. They would therefore be expected to enjoy a faster growth than the more mature economies of the north, and wages and living standards would rise accordingly. From a practical perspective, too, it was expected that firms operating across lots of different countries in Europe would find it difficult to pay workers markedly less in different places for any length of time given the greater transparency that a single currency generates. So rising relative wages in the periphery countries were inevitable. But if, at the same time, public or private investment in those countries is at insufficient levels, or has an insufficiently high rate of return to produce productivity gains, then it is obvious that unit labour costs would also rise relative to, say, Germany. And this is precisely what happened.

The second option, of course, would have been external devaluation, i.e. letting the currency's value fall and restoring competitiveness that way. Given the single currency this is clearly not an option any more. Instead what is required is internal devaluation (a fall in the unit labour costs). I have seen estimates suggesting that a reduction in relative prices of up to 30% may be required for Greece to regain its competitiveness with Germany. This could be achieved if inflation was allowed to rise sharply in Germany or the Germans suddenly decided to pay themselves more for the same, or less, effort (e.g. by cutting working hours without wage compensation), or if the Germans went on a spending spree – the problem is that this is not the behaviour that got them where they are. So the Greeks and others in this position have no other option but to restore competitiveness through nominal deflation – cutting costs (and hence wages) in money terms, with all the misery that this entails.

This book has provided some potent examples of what internal devaluation, structural adjustment and austerity programmes mean for the livelihoods and lives of the citizens of those countries now caught in this position. Despite an increasing number of reports and exposés featuring in the international media, the sheer misery being imposed is not fully appreciated by many political and bureaucratic leaders around Europe. And in my view, misery is not an overblown word. There will be a limit to how much austerity the populations of the peripheral economies can bear. At some point, in one or more countries, the politicians may decide the game is up and that exiting the euro is the 'least worst' outcome – or the voters may take matters into their own hands and throw out any politicians who want to stick with the euro.

WOULD GREECE BE BETTER OFF OUTSIDE THE EURO?

Exiting would be traumatic for any country. Even the suspicion that a country might exit the euro would lead to capital flight. Individuals would try and get their money out of the country or at least into some asset that could not be devalued at a stroke by the creation of a new currency. Greek banks have seen a significant outflow of deposits and it seems no coincidence that adverts have started appearing in the *Athens News*, an English-language Greek daily, for residential property in Denmark – a country that has weathered the crisis reasonably well and is outside the eurozone, even if the Danish crown is pegged to the euro and its exchange rate never varies! A serious possibility of exit – and how could it be kept completely secret? – would lead to a full-scale run on the banks. Clearly any country wishing to exit the eurozone would have to nationalise or take temporary control of the banks and reintroduce controls on the movement of capital. The government would also need to reintroduce stringent border controls to stop people leaving the country with euro notes and coins in their luggage or in their underwear! In countries like Greece, where taking to the streets is part of the political way of life, the population would probably react by attempting to physically remove their savings, breaking into the banks – and then for good measure attacking Parliament. So in Greece a euro exit could easily end with troops on the streets and martial law – just the circumstances that joining the EU was meant to prevent. Exiting the euro would also be accompanied by at least a partial default on external debts. An inability to access external finance markets would result in a trip to the printing presses and inevitable inflation.

An exit would also have costs to those remaining in the eurozone. There is the immediate risk of another financial crisis arising from contagion, as those banks with significant exposure to any country leaving the single currency would be faced with potentially massive losses. One country leaving would raise the possibility of another country leaving, leading to increased costs of borrowing for those countries the markets think most likely to leave next, with the risk that those countries then fulfill the prophecy. And we could guarantee that the general uncertainty and pessimism would lead to reduced business, consumer and investor confidence, prolonging the period of low growth.

WHAT NEEDS TO CHANGE?

There are good economic reasons why the eurozone leaders want to stick together apart from political sentiment. But, beyond just wishing that the eurozone can stay together, it requires further change over and above what is planned in the new treaty, as we have already seen with the political agreement reached at the June 2012 summit which strengthened support mechanisms for banking systems as well as establishing greater cross-national supervision of banks. So what further changes are required?

First, there need to be robust arrangements to help member states that run into difficulty. As the IMF put it in its five-point plan of mid-July 2012, it is essential to have demand support and crisis management in the short term to cushion the impact of adjustment efforts and maintain orderly market conditions – which, as we have recently seen in the case of Spain and Italy, can easily get out of hand. A stabilisation facility is needed that is big enough to cope with liquidity or financial crises in one of the larger economies such as Spain or Italy. The current stabilisation facilities can potentially raise up to €1trn, but even this sum might not be enough to stand behind both.

There also needs to be a mechanism for dealing

with crises of solvency, where the issue is the inability to pay debts rather than a shortage of funds. In these cases, while an injection of cash may be necessary to ensure that debt payments are met and the country continues to pay wages etc., the support needed might be more than that. It may well, as in the case of Greece, require some partial debt forgiveness. A stable future for the eurozone will also inevitably require its members to stand behind individual countries' debts. Again, this is an area where the IMF has suggested that automatic stabilisers should be allowed to operate fully. And considering the large downside risks that exist, it believes that strong, surplus countries in the region should be ready to assist through fiscal expansion themselves if such risks materialise.

Further help can be provided in a variety of ways. One is through the ECB buying sovereign debt in the secondary market, which it has done before and which it could be doing again in order to bring yields down at moments of crisis. It became obvious in mid to late July 2012 that the circumstances for an intervention through a securities purchase programme exactly a year earlier were repeating themselves, only in a more intense way. They now threatened Spain and Italy, which, if either country was forced to go for full-blown bail-outs, would severely test the eurozone firepower. Yields had to come down fast and the ECB finally intervened, with the full blessing of its paymasters, notably Germany. Rates duly came down and although there has been a series of crises reflecting political uncertainty since, yields on Italian and Spanish bonds in late August 2013, at around 4.5%, though slightly higher than earlier in the year, were still well down from the crisis levels of 7% and higher in 2012, when the ECB had to intervene in the markets.

The second way is by acting as sovereign lender of last resort, or more explicitly through the issue of Eurobonds. This is heavily contested; France wants Eurobonds, Germany is vehemently opposed as it doesn't want to be bearing the full brunt of keeping 'profligate' countries, as it sees them, afloat. The Germans have similar concerns with the proposed 'banking union' where again they fear that they may be left supporting weaker banks in Europe.

But, things are moving on apace and Germany may be unable to resist for much longer, however much it tries to hide behind its constitutional court. Timing here is important. With the ECB becoming the banking regulator in a new banking union, the European Stability Mechanism (ESM) may well develop in such a way as to be able both to lend/invest directly into the banking system as well as use ECB funding to invest directly in new issues of sovereign debt across the eurozone.

But as we get closer to banking and fiscal union the richer countries will end up inevitably covering and guaranteeing the poorer countries' debts. The discussion has now reached this stage but at the moment there is a very clear difference of view, with Germany implacably opposed to the pooling (or 'mutualisation') of debts and many other countries, not surprisingly, in favour. All sorts of options have been discussed as compromise solutions, including partial Eurobonds to cover up to 60% of the country's debt-to-GDP ratio with the rest left to domestic markets or a different system of individual country interest payments into the Eurobond system which would depend on those countries meeting various fiscal conditions. But it seems to me that whatever shape they eventually take Eurobonds will inevitably form part of the package. The Germans remain worried about the costs that they may have to shoulder but it is more than likely that the very existence of Eurobonds, if we ever get there, will have a calming influence on the markets, reduce the incidence of crises of confidence and also lower those costs substantially.

At the same time though, and in order to stop the problem getting worse, the less competitive economies need to increase their productivity – and at a faster rate than the Germans. This means more productive investment, probably involving some element of fiscal transfer by using the EU's structural funds and the capital available to the European Investment Bank more effectively. But there also needs to be real progress on structural reform. The bail-out packages to date have delivered more on austerity than structural reform, as acknowledged in the case of Greece by the head of the IMF delegation to Greece, Paul Thomsen, at a debate in 2012 at the LSE. There is no doubt that more time needs to be given to the Greeks to effect change as it is obvious from the various reports from the OECD, Transparency International and the European Commission that ability to implement change is limited at present and requires a huge amount of technical assistance to alter the current system, which is still corrupt and inefficient. It takes time for cultures to change and it's not only Greece – the periphery countries share many similar characteristics.

But ultimately the Germans will have to become a bit more like the Greeks – rather than simply the Greeks becoming like the Germans. It is of course a fallacy, as I have pointed out earlier, that the Greeks work much less hard than northern Europeans – in fact they are at the top of the league in terms of recorded working hours with the Germans at the bottom! But Germany needs to also recognise that it, and other nations running up surpluses within the eurozone, have to spend more of those surpluses on imported goods and services (or on longer holidays in southern Europe) to avoid or at least mitigate the structural imbalances within the eurozone.

And finally, progress towards a banking union must be speeded up. It had been taken for granted that the single market had delivered freedom of movement for capital. The financial crisis demonstrated that, while capital may be free to move across borders, it could actually do quite a lot of harm if it is allowed to create bubbles in an unregulated way. Also, money will not flow through Europe if the banking system dries up and makes it risky to borrow, lend or invest in other countries away from one's own national regulations and national systems of protection, such as deposit guarantees. There will be no inter-bank transfers if banks stop trusting each other and no financing of trade, which countries like Greece so desperately now need. Policy makers have taken some time to recognise the significance of this element of eurozone reform but, partly because the Commission had already been active in this area, it looks like we may see rapid progress.

This is an area where again the IMF has made strong recommendations. It suggested that Europe should show 'a credible commitment towards a robust and complete monetary union'. The elements of this should be a process for achieving a unified bank supervisory framework, a pan-European deposit insurance guarantee scheme and a unified bank resolution mechanism. It urged wide-ranging structural reforms throughout the eurozone to support the viability of the monetary union as it would help resolve intra-area current account imbalances, which, as mentioned earlier, have been a drag on growth. In mid-2013, the IMF was encouraging faster progress towards a banking union and greater efforts to resolve the lack of credit availability to companies, particularly SMEs.

WILL IT BE ACHIEVED?

This is an ambitious shopping list. It may of course have implications for the UK as we could be seeing a stronger more unified Europe while the UK remains a reluctant semi-detached participant from the outside. But importantly for Europe it will require voters in some countries to see much larger proportions of their (hard-earned) incomes being transferred to countries with lower standards of living that may be seen as the result of laziness, profligacy and (at best) a lack of will to take tough decisions. It would require voters in other countries having to accept radical changes to the structure of their economies and societies, including major redistributions of income and wealth. Although most of the population of the eurozone no doubt want it to stay together, it is less clear whether they would be prepared to accept these changes. So there is a real political question here: will the élite wedded to the euro persuade their voters to pool enough sovereignty and wealth to keep the eurozone intact? For that they will need to show that they and their economies will be better off staying in than facing the alternative.

The problem, however, is that the crisis has made the politics of further integration more, not less, difficult. We are seeing nationalism emerging more strongly practically everywhere. Throughout Europe there is now a growing political sentiment that attaches more weight to the economic interests of the nation state and less weight to the collective interests of Europe, the opposite of what has sometimes been termed 'solidaristic' behaviour. Even in 'rich' countries there is a rise in support for political parties that are sceptical about the EU or have turned against supporting 'profligate' foreign governments, such as the True Finns party in Finland and the Party for Freedom in the Netherlands. At a more extreme level, we have seen this lead to vilification of Germany. In Greece, swastika cartoons are now commonplace, while the neo-Nazi Golden Dawn party has emerged as a political force and entered Parliament.

As yet there has been no compelling and intellectually coherent vision of how democracy and accountability will be preserved – let alone enhanced – if the eurozone moves closer to a fiscal and political union. Ideas are tossed around, such as a directly elected President of Europe. Yet, to take this as an example, it has not been explained how this role would interact with that of President of the Commission, President of the Council or President of the Eurogroup. There is talk of involving national parliaments more in decision making but it is not at all clear how this is to be done. What the voters do see is the potential for European institutions to impose their will on democratically elected national governments. This is all too apparent to the Greeks, some of whom will feel that other governments and the troika have paid no attention to the message implicit in the results of last year's elections. But it would become more widespread if, for example, a future European Treasury were to veto the budget of a member state that was in no imminent financial difficulty and tell it to make spending cuts – or else. The question at this point is: or else what? In practice, the answer will depend on how large and powerful the member state in question is.

We saw that in Ireland when the country's MPs were shocked to discover that a constitutional finance committee of the German Parliament was able to look at the measures proposed by the Irish government in its budget due to be delivered in December 2011 before they had a chance to hear themselves of the VAT changes and other measures contained in it! A similar situation happened in Greece when the papers in Athens, under headlines screaming 'Who Runs Greece?', reported that the Bundestag in Germany had been discussing the details of a possible third package for Greece which the German Finance Minister stated need not be higher than €4–4.5bn. Not only was this much less than what the IMF believed was needed to close the funding gap, but all this was being discussed without the knowledge of the Greek Parliament.

Having said this, I do not feel we are at political crisis point – yet. The mood of the population is probably not anti-euro enough in sufficient member states that count. This latter point is an interesting judgement to make in itself. Three years ago who would have assumed that anyone would be watching the Greek election results on tenterhooks apart from the Greeks themselves? But Merkel and Hollande clearly have different philosophical viewpoints and appear to have reached different conclusions about the pace and sequencing of integration. For Merkel, collective backing of national borrowing is something to consider after the necessary supranational controls have been put in place to ensure fiscal rigour at the national level. It probably would be needed only if a country landed in trouble through some unexpected event that could not be countered by a tightening of the purse strings. For Hollande, collective backing for national borrowing is a pre-condition for the surrender of national sovereignty implicit in the budget control frameworks demanded by the Germans, something that will be resisted by most French voters. Nevertheless, it is in both their personal and national interests to save the euro from collapse – it cements the Franco-German axis as the single most important relationship in the EU. If it were a difference between France and Germany that fails to keep the euro together, would the EU take them as seriously about anything else?

WHAT'S NEXT?

The crisis in Europe is not over by any means. The calmness of the markets for most of 2013 hides the fact that the fundamentals have barely changed. In some cases they have worsened. As David Marsh explains in his latest book, Europe's Deadlock published in July 2013, years of continued mismanagement by Europe's leaders have made the contradictions at the heart of the European project more and more obvious. His view is that technical fixes alone will not solve the problem.

There is only one answer. For the periphery countries and Greece in particular, more debt will need to be written off and the periods over which fiscal consolidation needs to be achieved will probably have to be extended again. By way of recognising that this debt is unsustainable, there should be a further 'haircut', applying not only to the official holders of Greek sovereign debt but perhaps also that held by other countries. The ECB should be allowed, despite objection from some German quarters, to use the 'outright monetary transactions' (OMT) mechanism (introduced with such fanfare last year but not used so far) to buy up government bonds in the secondary markets and possibly other privately held assets and use this as a way to move rates down permanently and ease the pressure on Italy and Spain where even the lower interest rates on their debt they enjoyed for most of 2013 are unsustainable if their economies are not growing. What it requires in other words is for the ECB to use OMT to effectively engage in its own 'quantitative easing', a mechanism successfully in my view used in the US and the UK. And this is a good time to do it as despite signs of a tentative upturn in eurozone activity since the spring of 2013, the improvement is not uniform across all countries and there is a lot of spare capacity around to reassure Germany that any inflation fears implied by any relaxation would be unfounded. German inflation itself, despite the recent reappearance of growth, is forecast at only around 1.5% for this year and for 2014. Eurozone inflation in mid 2013 was running at just over 1%, well below the 2% level which is what the ECB believes denotes price stability and was one reason behind the ECB interest rate cut in mid 2013. Indeed Christine Lagarde said in late August 2013, just as the data was beginning to show some recovery, that in her view this was not the time to reverse loose monetary policies in many places around the world and there was still mileage from continuing what she called 'unconventional monetary policies in places like Europe'.

But the upshot is that Germany will have to accept that it needs to pay a large share of what is required to keep the system going. In a way, it should repay some of the economic benefits it has reaped from being in the euro – not only in terms of trade going in its direction from the periphery countries for much of the period but also from a euro that is much weaker and hence more competitive than it would have been were these problematic periphery countries not members of the eurozone. This would allow the crisis countries to breathe again and growth to restart though it would also require a much-needed injection of structural and technical funds. The German leadership would also have to explain properly and firmly to its population the benefits of the euro to Germany and the immense costs of a break-up against continuing and in some cases enhancing support for crisis countries.

But in return, countries such as Spain and Italy will need to accept that for that support the conditionality has to be significant. Reforms will have to happen, even though in retrospect they should never have been asked to implement them in such a hurry. Greece's request to delay the fiscal consolidation period by an extra two years, which was granted in November 2012, makes sense in this context. At the same time, though, the deep imbalances that the euro has created would have to be reversed. Germany will need to spend more and allow inflation to rise. The other countries should be allowed to benefit from a relative improvement in their competitiveness. For Germany that should make sense. The alternative – of them being left on their own or with a small group of like-minded or dependent countries that would then recreate the strong Deutschmark – would wipe out most profits from the German exporters and plunge the country back to the time when analysts and commentators were openly disparaging of its economic performance.

Of course not all countries need exactly the same type of support. Ireland may well emerge from its current predicament in a reasonably healthy position – possibly healthier for having learned that the gains from an overheated and imbalanced economy are transitory.

But still, growth in this export-dependent economy fell from 2.2% in 2011 to 0.2% in 2012 and GDP has contracted each quarter since the middle of last year. Before the latest output data for the second quarter of 2013 were announced, the Irish central bank had already reduced its growth forecasts for 2013 to 0.7% from over 1% earlier in the year but still expects growth of 2.1% next year. If this does not materialise Ireland will continue to have difficulty containing its budget deficit which despite a series of austerity measures, possibly with more to come in its forthcoming budget due in October 2013, is swollen by high interest payments on its debt. And unemployment in Ireland is likely to remain stubbornly high at over 13.5%. And the rest of the periphery countries may be just as unlucky.

THE FEAR OF CONTAGION

The concern among the eurozone leaders – and European and G20 leaders more generally – about Greece or one of the other smaller economies such as Portugal leaving the euro has not just been because of the costs of exit, substantial though these may be. It is also because one exit would, in the eyes of the markets, increase the probability of other countries exiting as the euro will prove 'reversible' – and would turn the attention to the other 'periphery' economies. We have seen how the Cyprus crisis in March 2013, despite the small size of its economy (some 0.2% of Europe's GDP), hugely affected markets across the eurozone amidst concerns about Cyprus' contin-ued viability within the euro area and fears that the recipe imposed on Cyprus, penalising depositors and nearly causing bank runs, could be replicated in other countries seeking further financial assistance from the troika. Spain (and undoubtedly also Italy if upward pressure on its sovereign bond yields had remained) are keen to avoid applying for a bail-out on similar terms to Greece, Ireland and Portugal – or for that matter Cyprus. No doubt there is an element on their part of national pride and reluctance, as big beasts within the eurozone, to be dictated to by the troika of the Commission, the ECB and the IMF. The bail-out facilities developed to date would struggle to accommodate a full-scale rescue of Spain or Italy – and they certainly could not cope with having to support both countries at the same time unless the mere fact of going for a bail-out helps to calm the markets.

That may happen. The agreement at the June 2012 European summit was to provide support for the banking sector directly from the ESM through injection of equity or bond purchases rather than via national governments, who then seek funding from the troika, which might reduce the risk of either of these countries having to seek a comprehensive bail-out and agree to new fiscal consolidation and structural reform programmes. In effect this recognised the original decision taken in June to provide support for Spanish banks directly rather than through the government. In addition, the push for the ESM to obtain a banking licence so it can intervene more directly in the bond markets by tapping ECB funds would add considerably to any possible intervention required in the future. This is all welcome. But it would clearly have been much better if that had been agreed and put into operation earlier as it would have calmed the markets and helped mitigate the spread of the crisis that we have seen from the smaller periphery countries to the bigger ones too. In any case, this mechanism will take time to implement as a permanent fixture because it nominally requires the ECB to take over supervisory responsibility for the European banking sector first.

Although the ECB did take on this role nominally from January 2013, the direct supervision of the banks in the eurozone countries and in those that decide to join the euro in the future will not start until 2014. There has been a lot of wrangling between countries as to which banks will be covered by this, given that the German government does not want to see 430 local *Sparkassen* (savings banks), their cooperative banks and their ten *Landesbanken* (regional banks) covered by the new regime. One suspects that this is because those organisations are all in reality used as a policy tool to help the economy and channel funds to SMEs, which are very important for the German economy. Whatever the reason, it now looks as if it will be the largest banks with assets of €30bn or more that will be directly supervised.

Not surprisingly there have been numerous calls from EU leaders, including from the UK but also the IMF and the US, for the whole process to be speeded up but the experience so far has been that things still take longer than the markets can bear. And 2013 saw yet more muddling through as the policy decisions of the previous year brought little respite. In July 2012 ECB President Mario Draghi said that the bank would 'do whatever it takes' to ensure the euro's survival. 'Believe me,' Mr Draghi added, 'it will be enough.' This bought time, as did the ECB's pledge to buy short-term government bonds from troubled countries under its so-called 'outright monetary transactions' (OMT) scheme – though the scheme hasn't been tested yet and the ECB hasn't paid anything out. By late 2013 too many banks were in a semi-zombie state. The banking crisis has not gone away and mutualisation of debt remains taboo.

But whatever happens in the short-term, Spain and Italy will continue to face difficulties in maintaining competitiveness with the more prosperous 'northern' member states. Spain, in particular, saw a substantial increase in its exports in 2012, but much of the improvement in 2013 has been due to lower imports as consumers have cut back. Italy has a high debt-to-GDP ratio of over 120%, which is potentially unsustainable and a reflection of the spendthrift habits of previous governments – although Spain's ratio has in the past been more comfortable, it has doubled from its pre-crisis levels to just under 90% in 2012 and it could well reach 100% in 2013. In reality therefore, both governments have problems in managing their public finances in the short and the long term. In Spain, a large part of public spending is channelled through the autonomous regions, and the government has found it difficult to keep their spending in check. The long-term cost of pensions is a problem in both countries. Both countries also need to make their labour markets more flexible and increase entrepreneurship and competition.

But more importantly both countries will find it difficult to sustain their debt if their economies continue to shrink. The Italians have been in this danger zone for some time, as they have seen very little growth in GDP over the last decade. The only relief had been the very low interest rates they enjoyed for most of that period so the debt-servicing burden was manageable. With growth prospects disappearing in the short and medium term this becomes seriously problematic. Indeed, for a long period Italy, despite its prosperous and productive north, was often considered by many economists to be the most dangerous piece of the entire eurozone jigsaw puzzle, briefly obscured by other countries like Greece and Ireland getting into more spectacular difficulties over the last couple of years. The Italian political system, in particular, has a track record of failing to deliver needed change, even with supposedly stable governments, which is one reason why Mario Monti's government of technocrats was appointed to push through necessary reforms. The coalition government that followed was headed by Enrico Letta – though 25% of Italian voters preferred the eccentric anti-EU Five Star Movement headed by former comedian, Beppe Grillo. Letta, a young centrist, visited London in July 2013 to insist that Italy was taking the right decisions. Nonetheless, those with vested interests, including Italy's 240,000 lawyers, universities that refused to employ European professors on the same basis as Italian nationals and pharmacies with high-price monopolies on basic drugs like aspirins, continue to resist competition and market-promoting reforms. Thus, although Italy managed in late May to extract itself from the European Commission's excessive deficit procedures that apply when deficits are over 3% of GDP, by getting its figures to be just under, the Commission still warned that many reforms still needed to be made with Italy's debt level remaining the second highest in Europe after Greece.

ALL IN THE SAME BOAT

The financial position of many banks in Europe remains a major concern and will continue to be a drag on growth prospects – and this is the case across Europe, not just Greece or even Ireland and Spain. The reality is that the system is interconnected; the French and German banks invested heavily in banks in the periphery countries and also engaged in direct private and government lending. And even that understates the linkages in the system: German banks lend to French banks that then lend to Greece/Ireland/Spain etc. and then they all come down together. Banks across Europe have had to deal with the aftermath of a banking crisis that has left them with huge write-offs and continuing underperforming loans, and in addition they have been holding increasing amounts of their own national government debt, encouraged to do so by the huge expansion of the liquidity that the ECB has made available to the banks (LTRO). Many of these problems are only surfacing now, the July 2012 Spanish banking rescue being a good example. Without a properly functioning banking system Europe will enter an even deeper recession. It is the drying up of liquidity that is feared most. The cleaning up of the banks is always going to be a long process and the move to a banking union is very much part of this.

With the recession that has followed this has clearly ceased to be a Greek problem but one that is familiar across Europe. The EU leaders have to adapt their thinking to the realities of these countries and the fact that austerity alone will not solve the problem but will make it worse. They need to recognise that in the process of not listening and not getting it, they have allowed a fully fledged banking crisis to come along which has affected every angle of the European economy and necessitated increasing sums of money to douse the fire. The bail-outs of the countries have in reality been bail-outs of the banking system across Europe as a whole as it was being threatened with collapse at various stages over the last two years.

So whatever its original flaws, the best way forward is for the euro to survive. A Greek exit would raise serious concerns about contagion, and worries about the future are at present affecting confidence and investors' willingness to put money into the eurozone. But there is no logic in going back. The cost to Europe of letting Greece go rather than staying in the euro will be much greater and the funds that will be needed after a Greek exit to calm the markets will be prohibitive. It is a sign of how damaging the prevarication of politicians has been that the casting aside of a country that does not fit the pattern any more might be seen as a way forward rather than a terrible backward step. When the Cyprus crisis erupted in March 2013, it was the same story. Prolonged and badly executed negotiations for a small – by European standards – bail-out of around €10bn threatened once again to destabilise the whole euro project and demonstrated to all the lack of strategic perspective among EU leaders.

EURO SURVIVAL

Greece is in a position now where the new government has no choice but to implement reform; its survival depends on it. Greece has to learn to live by the injunction of the Delphi Oracle: 'Know thyself'. Greece, or rather the Greek élites, have refused to know themselves, to accept responsibility for the many failings in the stewardship of the nation. Politicians, professionals, prelates and power interest groups like parties, employers and unions have all been in denial for too long. But so have the leaders of the rest of Europe. Yes, the economies have to restructure, open up and become more competitive. And indeed there has to be more shared responsibility for budgets to avoid a similar crisis again soon. And yes, there has to be better banking supervision and regulators need to up their game. But there will also need to be agreement that the debts need to be written off and that the pain also needs to be shared. It is in every eurozone country's long-term political and economic interest to be part of a vibrant and growing Europe. As Angela Merkel says: 'If the euro fails, Europe fails.' There are some who want to see the euro and the EU break up. It is difficult to see how this can benefit Greece. Merkel now has the chance to show if she and Germany can provide the leadership to ensure that neither the EU nor its single currency fail. On 22 September 2013, she won a handsome victory to remain Chancellor of Germany for a third term. Her victory was spoiled, however, by the defeat of her centre-right partner, the liberal Free Democratic Party, which failed to get enough votes to enter the Bundestag. A majority of Germans voted for left-of-centre parties which have been critical of the hard austerity measures Brussels has imposed across Europe. In the summer of 2014, Europe has to choose a new parliament, a new Commission and elect presidents to the European Council, the European Commission, the European Parliament and the Eurogroup. Soon Europe will have new leadership and a changed government in Germany. Whether the new leaders of Europe can rise to the challenge of finding effective ways out of the crisis remains an open question.

Greece should play its part in the euro's survival. It won't be easy and there will be a mountain to climb, especially as Greece's credibility with its own people and the people of Europe is at its lowest. Greece will have to convince the creditors that it can deliver on its promises but Prime Minister Samaras has persuaded EU leaders to grant an extension on the schedule for reforms for the second bail-out package. He, like everyone else, now knows that continued aid to Greece will be results oriented, particularly when it comes to effecting structural reforms and implementing deficit-reducing measures. But the prize on all sides is worth the effort. The alternative could well be chaos.

Greece is part of the Balkans, Europe's south-east flank. The Balkans needs to be Europeanised. The alternative – the Balkanisation of Europe – is to return the continent to its far from happy past.

GLOSSARY

Agency Workers Directive:
A European Union directive agreed in November 2008 that seeks to guarantee those working through employment agencies equal pay and conditions with employees in the same business who do the same work.

ATM:
Automatic teller machine.

Austerity:
Refers to a policy of deficit cutting by lowering spending, often via a reduction in the amount of benefits and public services provided.

Bail-out:
A loan to a company or country that faces serious financial difficulty or bankruptcy.

Banco de España:
The Bank of Spain is the national central bank of Spain.

Bank of England:
The central bank of the United Kingdom.

Bank of Greece:
The national central bank of Greece, located in Athens.

Bankia:
A Spanish banking conglomerate.

Banque de France: The central bank of France.

BBVA: Banco Bilbao Vizcaya Argentaria, a multinational Spanish banking group.

Black Wednesday: Refers to the events of 16 September 1992 when the British Conservative government was forced to withdraw the pound sterling from the European Exchange Rate Mechanism (ERM) after it was unable to keep it above its agreed lower limit.

Bloomberg: Bloomberg LP is an American multinational mass media corporation based in New York.

Bretton Woods system: A system of monetary management, it established the rules for commercial and financial relations among the world's major industrial states in the mid-twentieth century.

Bundesrat: The legislative body of Germany.

Bundesver-fassungsgericht: The German federal constitutional court.

Cabinet: The collective decision-making body of the government of the United Kingdom, composed of the Prime Minister and some twenty-two Cabinet Ministers, the most senior of the government ministers.

Common Agricultural Policy: CAP, a system of European Union agricultural subsidies and programmes.

Capital Economics:	A leading independent macroeconomic research consultancy.
CEO:	Chief executive officer.
CER:	Centre for European Reform, a London-based think tank devoted to improving the quality of the debate on the future of the European Union.
CFDT:	Confédération Française Démocratique du Travail or French Democratic Confederation of Labour, one of the five national trade union confederations of France.
CFSI:	Centre for Financial Services Innovation.
CGT:	Confédération Générale du Travail or General Confederation of Labour, one of the five national trade union confederations of France.
Christian Democratic Union:	CDU, a Christian democratic and liberal-conservative political party in Germany.
Christian Social Union of Bavaria:	CSU, a Christian democratic and conservative political party in Germany.
City of London:	London's major business and financial centre.
Commerzbank:	A German global banking and financial services company.
Common Market:	An initial stage towards a single market.
Commons Treasury Select Committee:	A Select Committee of the House of Commons in the Parliament of the United Kingdom.

Congress: The bicameral legislature of the federal government of the United States, consisting of the Senate, its upper house, and the House of Representatives, its lower house.

Conservative Party: Officially the Conservative and Unionist Party, a centre-right political party in the United Kingdom that adheres to the philosophies of conservatism and British unionism.

Credit default swap: CDS is a financial swap agreement, where the seller of the CDS will compensate the buyer in the event of a loan default or other credit event. The buyer of the CDS makes a series of payments (the CDS 'fee' or 'spread') to the seller and, in exchange, receives a payoff if the loan defaults.

Debt-to-GDP ratio: The amount of national debt of a country as a percentage of its gross domestic product (GDP) and one of the indicators of the health of an economy.

Delocalisation: Relocating production to another country.

Deutsche Bundesbank: The German Federal Bank, the central bank of the Federal Republic of Germany.

DIMAR: A democratic socialist and social-democratic political party in Greece.

DM:	Deutschmark, was the official currency of West Germany (1948–1990) and Germany (1990–2002) until the adoption of the euro in the 2002 Exchange Rate Mechanism (ERM).
DTI:	The Department of Trade and Industry within the United Kingdom government.
EC:	European Commission, the executive body of the European Union.
ECB:	European Central Bank.
ECFR:	European Council for Foreign Relations.
ECOFIN:	Economic and Financial Affairs Council.
École Nationale d'Administration:	ENA, one of the most prestigious of French graduate schools.
EEC:	European Economic Community, also known as the Common Market.
EFSF:	European Financial Stability Facility.
Élysée Treaty:	Also known as the Treaty of Friendship, concluded by Charles de Gaulle and Konrad Adenauer in 1963. It sealed reconciliation between Germany and France.
EMU:	European Monetary Union.
Énarques:	Graduates from the ENA.
ESM:	European Stability Mechanism.
EU:	European Union.
EU Task Force:	The Task Force is a resource at the disposal of the Greek authorities as they seek to build a modern and prosperous Greece.

Euro:	The official currency of the eurozone.
Eurobond:	Bonds issued outside the jurisdiction of a firm's domestic market but now increasingly referred to as jointly issued debt instruments by the eurozone.
Eurogroup:	A meeting of the finance ministers of the eurozone.
European Coal and Steel Community:	ECSC, a six-nation international organisation serving to unify democratic countries of Europe during the Cold War and create the foundation for the modern-day developments of the European Union.
European Council:	An institution of the European Union, comprising the heads of state or government of the EU member states, along with the President of the European Commission and the President of the European Council.
European Investment Bank:	The European Union's long-term lending institution established in 1958 under the Treaty of Rome.
European Parliament:	The directly elected parliamentary institution of the European Union.
European People's Party:	A centre-right European political party. The EPP was founded in 1976 by Christian democratic parties, but later increased its membership to include conservative parties and parties of other centre-right perspectives.

Euroscepticism: The body of criticism towards the European Union.

Eurozone: An economic and monetary union (EMU) of seventeen European Union (EU) member states that have adopted the euro (€) as their common currency and sole legal tender. The eurozone currently consists of Austria, Belgium, Cyprus, Estonia, Finland, France, Germany, Greece, Ireland, Italy, Luxembourg, Malta, the Netherlands, Portugal, Slovakia, Slovenia and Spain.

Fédéraste: A derogatory term used to attack supporters of European federalism, invented by Jean-Marie Le Pen.

Financial transaction tax: A levy placed on a specific type of monetary transaction for a particular purpose.

Fiscal union: The integration of the fiscal policy of nations or states.

FO: Force Ouvrière or General Confederation of Labour is one of the five national trade union confederations of France.

Free Democratic Party: Abbreviated to FDP, a classical liberal political party in Germany.

Front National: An extreme right-wing nationalist political party in France.

G20:	A group of twenty finance ministers and central bank governors from twenty major economies (nineteen countries plus the European Union).
GDP:	Gross domestic product, the market value of all officially recognised final goods and services produced within a country in a given period.
Golden Dawn party:	A right-wing extremist political organisation in Greece.
Goldman Sachs:	An American multinational investment banking firm.
Grexit:	A term used to describe the possible Greek exit from the euro.
Gross value added:	A measure in economics of the value of goods and services produced in an area, industry or sector of an economy.
Hartz reforms:	A set of recommendations that resulted from a commission on reforms to the German labour market in 2002.
House of Commons:	The lower house of the United Kingdom Parliament.
HRADF:	Hellenic Republic Assets Development Fund.
IFO Institute:	A Munich-based research institution, one of Germany's largest economic think tanks. IFO stands for Information und Forschung (research).
IMF:	International Monetary Fund.

Institute of
International
Finance:
The world's only global association of
financial institutions.

IOC: International Olympic Committee.

Junta: A government led by a committee of
military leaders.

KKE: The unreformed Communist Party of
Greece.

KPMG: One of the largest professional services
firms in the world.

Labour Party: The Labour Party is a centre-left
political party in the United Kingdom,
and one of the two main British
political parties along with the
Conservative Party.

Landesbanken: Regional banks of a type unique to
Germany.

Lehman Brothers: A global financial services firm that
declared bankruptcy in 2008.

LSE: London School of Economics.

LTRO: Long-term refinancing operations.

Maastricht Treaty: Formally the Treaty on European Union
or TEU, it was signed on 7 February
1992 by the members of the European
Community in Maastricht, the
Netherlands.

Maginot line: Named after the French Minister of
War André Maginot, this was a line
of concrete fortifications, tank obstacles,

	artillery casemates, machine gun posts, and other defences, that France constructed along its borders with Germany and Italy, in light of its experience in the First World War and in the run-up to the Second World War.
Marshall Plan:	Officially the European Recovery Program (ERP), the large-scale American programme to aid Europe where the United States gave monetary support to help rebuild European economies after the end of the Second World War in order to prevent the spread of Soviet Communism.
Member state:	A state that is party to treaties of the European Union (EU) and thereby subject to the privileges and obligations of EU membership.
MEP:	Member of the European Parliament.
Mittelstand:	A term to denote the collective of mid-sized companies in Germany which are the mainstay of the economy.
Moody's:	Moody's Investor Services, a credit ratings agency.
MP:	Member of Parliament.
National Economic Council:	A Cabinet advisory committee created by the UK government in 2008, replacing the Economic Development Committee.
NATO:	North Atlantic Treaty Organization.

NPV:	Net present value.
OECD:	Organisation for Economic Co-operation and Development.
OMFIF:	Official Monetary and Financial Institutions Forum.
Open Europe:	A think tank with offices in London and Brussels, promoting ideas for economic and political reform of the European Union.
Pasok:	The Panhellenic Socialist Movement, known mostly by its acronym, is the main centre-left party and, historically, one of the two major political parties in Greece.
PIIGS:	The term describing Portugal, Ireland, Italy, Greece and Spain.
PSI:	Private sector involvement.
R&D:	Research and development.
Re-Define:	An international think tank.
Santander:	A Spanish banking group.
SDOE:	The financial and economic crime unit of Greece.
Single European Act:	SEA, the first major revision of the 1957 Treaty of Rome. The Act set the European Community an objective of establishing a single market by 31 December 1992, and codified European Political Co-operation, the forerunner of the European Union's Common Foreign and Security Policy.

Single market: A type of trade bloc composed of a free trade area (for goods) with common policies on product regulation, and freedom of movement for the factors of production (capital and labour) and of enterprise and services.

Solidaristic: From the term 'solidarism' applied to the socio-political thought advanced by Émile Durkheim, which is loosely applied to a leading social philosophy operative during and within the French Third Republic prior to the First World War.

Stability and Growth Pact: An agreement made by the twenty-seven member states of the European Union, to facilitate and maintain the stability of the Economic and Monetary Union.

Structural funds: A financial tool set up to implement the cohesion policy, also referred to as the regional policy of the European Union.

Supranational: A type of multinational confederation or federation where negotiated power is delegated to an authority by governments of member states. The concept of supranational union is sometimes used to describe the European Union.

Supreme Court: The highest court in the United States.

Syriza: Coalition of the Radical Left, known mostly by its acronym 'Syriza', is a

	left-wing political party in Greece, originally founded as a coalition of left-wing and radical left political parties.
Syrtaki:	A popular dance of Greek origin, choreographed by Giorgos Provias for the 1964 film *Zorba the Greek*.
Think tank:	An organisation that conducts research and engages in advocacy in areas such as social policy, political strategy, economics, military and technological issues and in the creative and cultural field.
Trades Union Congress:	A federation of trade unions in the United Kingdom.
Treasury:	The United Kingdom government department responsible for developing and executing the British government's public finance policy and economic policy.
Treaty of Rome:	The treaty signed in 1957 establishing the European Economic Community (EEC) as a customs union on 1 January 1958.
Troika:	The tripartite committee led by the European Commission with the International Monetary Fund and the European Central Bank, which organised loans to the governments of Greece, Ireland and Portugal.
UK:	United Kingdom.
UKIP:	The United Kingdom Independence Party, a fiercely anti-European party led by Nigel Farage.

UMP:	The Union for a Popular Movement, a centre-right political party in France.
USA:	United States of America.
VAT:	Value added tax, a form of consumption tax.
'*Wirtschafts-wunder*':	German for 'economic miracle', describes the rapid reconstruction and development of the economies of West Germany and Austria after the Second World War.
Working Time Directive:	A European Union directive that creates the right for EU workers to a minimum number of holidays each year, paid breaks and rest of at least eleven hours in any twenty-four hours. It also restricts excessive night work and gives the default right to work no more than forty-eight hours per week.

CHRONOLOGY

This chronology is partial and selective and therefore does not claim to be complete, but does capture the main points regarding the creation of the euro and Greece's place within the eurozone.

Date	Event
1 March 1871	The French National Assembly supports a United States of Europe.
1923	Trotsky puts forward the slogan 'For a Soviet United States of Europe'.
1923	The Austrian Count Richard Coudenhove-Kalergi launches the Pan-Europa Movement.
1926	The First Paneuropean Congress is held in Vienna.
1931	Two books are published by French politician Édouard Herriot and English civil servant Arthur Salter, both entitled *The United States of Europe*.

9 September 1946	Winston Churchill talks of the 'United States of Europe' in a speech delivered at the University of Zürich, Switzerland.
14 May 1947	Under Winston Churchill, the United Europe Movement is created.
1 June 1947	The French economist and academic René Courtin creates the French Council for a United Europe, later integrated into the European Movement in 1953.
3 June 1947	The Socialist United States of Europe Movement is born, later renamed the European Left in 1961. Soon after, the Marshall Plan is launched to boost the European economy.
7–11 May 1948	The Europe Congress meets in The Hague, the Netherlands, headed by Winston Churchill with 800 delegates in attendance.
28 January 1949	France, the United Kingdom and the Benelux countries decide to establish a Council of Europe and ask Denmark, Ireland, Italy, Norway and Switzerland to assist with the preparation of the Council's statute.
5 May 1949	The statute is signed in London.
9 May 1950	French Foreign Minister Robert Schuman proposes an integration of the coal and steel industries of western Europe.

3 June 1950   Belgium, France, Luxembourg, Italy, the Netherlands and Germany sign up to the Schuman declaration.

August 1950   The Council of Europe Assembly approves the Schuman plan.

15 February 1951   Paris hosts a meeting about the creation of the European Community of Defence. Belgium, France, Italy, Luxembourg and Germany are in attendance with six other countries observing (USA, Canada, Denmark, Norway, the United Kingdom and the Netherlands).

April 1951   Belgium, France, Germany, Italy, Luxembourg and the Netherlands sign the Treaty of Paris to form the European Coal and Steel Community (ECSC).

27 May 1952   Belgium, France, Germany, Italy, Luxembourg and the Netherlands sign the European Defence Community (EDC) Treaty in Paris.

23 July 1952   The ECSC Treaty is launched. Jean Monnet, economist and diplomat who had also been Head of France's General Planning Commission, is appointed President of the High Authority and Paul-Henri Spaak, a former Belgian Prime Minister, President of the Common Assembly.

1 January 1953	The ECSC levy, the first European tax, comes into effect.
10 February 1953	The common market for coal and iron ore is put into place. Belgium, France, Germany, Italy, Luxembourg and the Netherlands remove customs duties and quantitative restrictions on coal and iron ore.
9 March 1953	Paul-Henri Spaak delivers a draft treaty to G. Bidault, President of the ECSC Council, instituting a political European community.
12 August 1953	The ECSC and the International Labour Organisation (ILO) sign an agreement of cooperation.
11 May 1954	Alcide de Gasperi, former Italian Prime Minister, is elected President of the European Parliamentary Assembly.
30 August 1954	The French National Assembly fails to ratify the EDC Treaty.
23 October 1954	Agreements on a modified Treaty are signed in Paris and the Western European Union (WEU) is born.
10 November 1954	Jean Monnet resigns from his post as President of the ECSC High Authority after the failure of the EDC.
1 June 1955	René Mayer, former French Prime Minister, is elected President of the ECSC High Authority.

8 December 1955	The Council of Europe launches the blue flag with twelve gold stars as its official emblem.
29 May 1956	Paul-Henri Spaak's report on the draft community treaties is approved. Intergovernmental negotiations begin to set up a European Economic Community and an Atomic Energy Community.
25 March 1957	The treaties establishing the European Economic Community (EEC) and the European Atomic Energy Community (Euratom) are signed by Belgium, France, Germany, Italy, Luxembourg and the Netherlands in Rome. They are thus referred to as the 'Treaties of Rome'.
19 March 1958	Robert Schuman is elected President of the European Parliamentary Assembly. This assembly substitutes for the ECSC Assembly.
8 June 1959	Greece applies for association with the EEC.
30 July 1962	The regulations creating a Common Agricultural Policy (CAP) enter into force, giving the countries joint control over food production. All farmers are to be paid the same price for their produce.

11 May 1967	The United Kingdom re-applies to join the EEC (after the French veto in 1963). It is followed by Ireland and Denmark and soon, by Norway.
29–30 May 1967	A summit celebrating the tenth anniversary of the signing of the EEC and Euratom Treaties is held in Rome.
1 July 1967	The Merger Treaty comes into effect, linking the executives of the European Communities (ECSC, EEC, Euratom). The European Communities now have a single Commission and a single Council.
1 July 1968	The customs union comes into effect.
26 November 1970	The Council announces reforms to the European Social Fund (ESF) in order to give the Community a suitable instrument for ensuring correlation between social policy and the other common policies.
22 January 1972	Denmark, Ireland, Norway and the United Kingdom sign the treaties to join the European Communities.
24 April 1972	The Exchange Rate Mechanism (ERM) is created. Belgium, France, Germany, Italy, Luxembourg and the Netherlands agree to limit the margin of fluctuation between their currencies to 2.25%.

10 May 1972   A referendum is held in Ireland on the country joining the European Communities. The majority vote in favour.

12 September 1972   The finance ministers of Belgium, France, Germany, Italy, Luxembourg, the Netherlands, Denmark, Ireland, Norway and the United Kingdom meet in Rome. They agree to establish a European Monetary Cooperation Fund.

25 September 1972   A referendum is held in Norway on the country joining the European Communities. The majority vote against.

2 October 1972   A referendum is held in Denmark on the country joining the European Communities. The majority vote in favour.

1 January 1973   Denmark, Ireland and the United Kingdom formally join the European Communities.

18 March 1975   The Council establishes the European Regional Development Fund (ERDF) and a Regional Policy Committee.

9 February 1976   The Council agrees on Greece's application for Community membership.

6 June 1978   The Council agrees on the membership application of Portugal and negotiations begin.

12–13 March 1979	A Council meeting is held in Paris. The European Monetary System (EMS), based on a European currency unit, the ECU, is established.
1 January 1981	Greece joins the European Communities.
18 October 1981	Legislative elections take place in Greece. The Greek people elect their members to the European Parliament.
1 January 1986	Spain and Portugal enter the European Communities, bringing membership to twelve.
9 November 1989	The collapse of Communism across Europe is symbolised by the fall of the Berlin Wall.
October 1990	Germany is united after more than forty years and the east of Germany joins the European Communities.
7 February 1992	The Treaty on European Union is signed in Maastricht. It defines rules for the future single currency and for foreign and security policy and closer cooperation in justice and home affairs. As part of the Treaty the European Communities become the European Union (EU).
31 July 1992	Greece approves the Treaty on the EU.
1 January 1993	The single market is established with the free movement of goods, services, people and money as its aim.

5 April 1994	Poland applies to join the EU.
1 January 1995	Austria, Finland and Sweden join the EU.
26 March 1995	Belgium, Germany, Spain, France, Luxembourg, the Netherlands and Portugal enforce the Schengen Agreement. This allows travel between all these countries without any passport control at the borders.
17 June 1997	The Treaty of Amsterdam is signed, amending the Maastricht Treaty.
13 December 1997	EU leaders agree to negotiate membership with twelve more European countries: Bulgaria, the Czech Republic, Estonia, Hungary, Latvia, Lithuania, Poland, Romania, Slovakia, Cyprus, Malta and Slovenia.
16 March 1998	The drachma enters the EMS Exchange Rate Mechanism (ERM).
3 May 1998	A special council agrees that eleven member states satisfy conditions for adoption of the single currency. The ministers and central bank governors of member states adopt the euro as their single currency.
1 January 1999	Belgium, Germany, Spain, France, Ireland, Italy, Luxembourg, the Netherlands, Austria, Portugal and Finland adopt the euro for commercial

and financial transactions only. Denmark, Sweden and the United Kingdom decide not to adopt the euro.

1 January 2001   Greece adopts the euro, becoming the twelfth member of the eurozone.

1 January 2002   Euro notes and coins enter circulation.

1 May 2004   The Czech Republic, Estonia, Latvia, Lithuania, Hungary, Poland, Slovenia, Slovakia, Cyprus and Malta join the EU.

23 September 2004   An investigation into Greece's national accounts show it joined the euro with a budget deficit above the 3% of gross domestic product limit set under the Stability and Growth Pact adopted by the EU in 1997.

29 October 2004   The twenty-five EU countries sign a treaty establishing a European Constitution. Its main aim is to speed up democratic decision making and management in the EU. The position of a European Foreign Minister is created.

1 January 2007   Bulgaria and Romania join the EU.

2007   The first signs of financial problems are spotted in the United States mortgage loan markets.

September 2008	The global financial crisis hits. Many European banks experience difficulties. The UK part-nationalises two major high street banks, in addition to the smaller Northern Rock, which was taken into public ownership the year before.
22 February 2009	European members of the G20 group agree to fight the financial crisis.
2 April 2009	London hosts the G20 summit, which agrees that €832bn will be put into the International Monetary Fund (IMF) and other financial institutions.
7 May 2009	The EU holds a special employment summit in Prague to tackle how the financial crisis is affecting the European job market.
5 November 2009	New Greek Prime Minister George Papandreou announces that Greece's 2009 budget deficit will be 12.7% of GDP. He says he will fight the nation's possible bankruptcy.
1 December 2009	The Lisbon Treaty comes into effect, amending the Maastricht Treaty and the Treaty of Rome, and creating the position of President of the European Council and a High Representative for Foreign Affairs and Security.

11 February 2010	Heads of state and government meet in Brussels to agree support for the Greek government to meet the country's stability programme targets for 2010.
26 March 2010	At a European Council meeting in Brussels, EU leaders adopt Europe 2020 targets and all sixteen eurozone countries get behind the plan to help Greece deal with its deficit.
2 May 2010	Greece agrees its first €110bn bail-out with the EU, the European Central Bank (ECB) and the International Monetary Fund, known as the 'troika', in return for extra budget cuts.
9 May 2010	The European Financial Stability Facility (EFSF), financed by the eurozone members and agreed by the twenty-seven member states, is agreed to promote financial stability.
29 October 2010	The Council discusses strengthening the eurozone and making economies less susceptible to economic crises.
28 November 2010	Ireland secures an €85bn bail-out.
1 January 2011	Three financial supervisory authorities are born: the European Banking Authority, the European Insurance and Occupational Pensions Authority and the European Securities and Markets Authority.

18 January 2011   The first 'European semester' gets underway – a six-monthly cycle of economic policy coordination between EU countries, which is meant to assist in the prevention of future economic crises.

25 March 2011   A comprehensive package (the Euro Plus Pact) to strengthen the economy is finalised at the European Council in Brussels.

16 May 2011   Eurozone heads approve a €78bn bail-out package for Portugal.

30 June 2011   The Greek Parliament agrees to spending cuts and structural reforms to reduce the country's debt.

11 July 2011   Eurozone countries sign a treaty creating a European Stability Mechanism (ESM), able to lend up to €500bn to eurozone countries in crisis.

October 2011   Eurozone leaders and the IMF agree €130bn of support measures to assist Greece, including a 'haircut' of 50% for private investors and €30bn to recapitalise Greek banks.

31 October 2011   Greek Prime Minister George Papandreou calls for a referendum on the EU bail-out deal for Greece.

2 November 2011   German Chancellor Angela Merkel and French President Nicolas Sarkozy hint for the first time that the

eurozone is prepared to move on without Greece, as they give Papandreou an ultimatum to ensure a yes on an austerity vote ahead of the G20 summit in Cannes.

10 November 2011   George Papandreou formally steps down as Greek Prime Minister and the referendum idea is abandoned due to the strong domestic and international negative reaction to it.

11 November 2011   New Greek Prime Minister Lucas Papademos (formerly Governor of the Central Bank of Greece and the ECB's Governing Council) leads a new technocratic coalition government with a mandate to negotiate the conditions for the second bail-out package.

2 February 2012   Second treaty to establish the European Stability Mechanism (ESM) is signed to replace the European Financial Stability Facility (EFSF) and the European Financial Stabilisation Mechanism (EFSM).

21 February 2012   Eurozone finance ministers agree on the terms of a second bail-out to secure Greece's future in the eurozone. The deal includes an agreement with private sector creditors on their Greek debts, with a marginally bigger 'haircut' of 53.5%.

1 March 2012	The European Council grants candidate status to Serbia.
29 March 2012	The European Parliament adopts laws making trade in over-the-counter (OTC) derivatives safer and more transparent.
6 May 2012	A general election is held in Greece. Results are inconclusive, with no party given a clear majority and a rise in support for extreme left- and extreme right-wing parties as a protest vote against the austerity measures.
16 May 2012	Greece announces new elections for 17 June after attempts to form a coalition government fail.
9 June 2012	Eurozone finance ministers agree a €100bn bank rescue package for Spain.
17 June 2012	Greece holds another general election, with the pro-austerity New Democracy party getting most votes, allaying fears of a Greek exit from the eurozone.
21 June 2012	A three-party coalition government is formed in Greece vowing to keep Greece in the eurozone with New Democracy, led by Prime Minister Antonis Samaras, teaming up with former opponents Pasok and the Democratic Left party.

25 June 2012	Cyprus becomes the fourth eurozone country to ask for a bail-out.
29 June 2012	An EU summit decides on a new 'Compact for Growth and Jobs' as the economic situation in the region continues to worsen. It also proposes to turn the ECB into a single banking authority and to allow the ESM to inject funds into banks directly. It is also decided that the combined EFSF and ESM funds could be used to buy countries' bonds and keep yields down, subject to meeting country-specific budget guidelines laid down by the European Commission.
9 July 2012	The newly formed Greek government wins a vote of confidence in the Greek Parliament, providing a mandate to tackle the country's ongoing financial problems and stay within the eurozone.
23 July 2012	The euro hits new lows and Spain's borrowing costs remain unsustainable, over fears the nation may need a complete bail-out.
27 July 2012	Antonis Samaras meets international creditors to try and persuade them that Athens deserves its final instalment of bail-out money. The EU, IMF and ECB examine Greece's finances before deciding whether to give €31.5bn.

22 August 2012	Antonis Samaras meets Jean-Claude Juncker, the President of the forum of the eurozone finance ministers, and opens discussions on having an extra two years to meet bail-out conditions. A package of further deficit reduction measures of €11.6bn is proposed by the Greek government.
24–25 August 2012	Antonis Samaras meets EU leaders to lay the ground for negotiations over a softening of terms. President Hollande and Chancellor Merkel set up a joint working group on the Greek crisis to monitor progress.
6 September 2012	The ECB announces its intention to engage in 'unlimited' purchases of short-term bonds in secondary markets of crisis countries, but only if they ask for formal bail-outs and subject to strict conditions.
12 September 2012	German Constitutional court approves the general principle of the ESM. EC President Barosso outlines proposals towards a banking union starting in January 2013.
28 September 2012	Spain unveils strict austerity budget to handle a deteriorating budget deficit and announces that its banks need some €59bn of recapitalisation money. Major bank restructuring follows.

8 October 2012	The eurozone permanent bail-out fund of €500bn, known as the European Stability Mechanism, is launched by eurozone finance ministers. It is to be used to help highly indebted countries coming under pressure from the markets.
November 2012	Greece is given two more years grace by the eurozone to meet deficit reduction targets.
27 November 2012	Greece to withdraw some €40bn of debt through negotiating a cut in the interest rate it pays on its rescue loans, agreeing with the ECB that any profits the central bank makes on the Greek debt it owns will be returned to Greece and through the Greek state being able to buy back debt from private investors at sharply reduced prices.
3 December 2012	Spain requests disbursement of €39.5bn from the €100bn made available to it in June to support and restructure its banking sector.
13 December 2012	European finance ministers agree to implement a 'Banking Union' across the eurozone to strengthen the banking sector. An agreement is made to create a common banking supervisor, which would be the ECB from January 2013. A common

resolution framework for banks in the eurozone and a common deposit guarantee scheme are also proposed.

15 March 2013   Portugal is given an extra year to reduce its deficit to less than 3% and the way is cleared for the country to receive next tranche of €2bn of bail-out funds.

28 March 2013   Cyprus agrees to a €10bn bail-out to prevent collapse of its banking system which had invested heavily in Greek sovereign bonds and in lending to the Greek private sector. A run on the banks as the Cypriots try to raise some €5.8bn through a levy on bank deposits is only avoided by forcing the banks to close for two weeks, through withdrawal limits and capital controls and by cancelling any losses on deposits of under €100,000.

2 April 2013   It is announced that the completion of the major recapitalisation of Greece's four large banks using bail-out funding will be delayed by a month. It finally occurs in June with the EFSF taking a large position in the four systemic banks left after absorbing the 'good part' of the smaller problem banks. Eurobank sees its main shareholder, Latsis,

pull out of the bank, which fails to raise the required Tier 1 capital and is now managed by the EFSF. The Greeks argue that the €50bn slated to recapitalise the banks should not count as a bail-out loan but, like in Spain, should be calculated separately, which would lower Greek indebtedness by 20%.

4 April 2013 — Concerns mount that Slovenia will be the next country after Cyprus to ask for an EU/IMF bail-out.

2 May 2013 — ECB cuts main interest rate by 0.25% to a record low 0.5% and announces that it is considering cutting the deposit rate it offers to banks to a negative one to encourage them to lend to SMEs instead.

11 May 2013 — Data on Greek GDP confirms that the economy contracted by 5.7% in Q4 2012, making it a decline of 6.4% for the year as a whole. This was the fifth year running that Greece saw its GDP decline.

29 May 2013 — France, Spain and Poland given two more years to reach the 3% deficit target and Belgium, Netherlands one extra year. Italy and Hungary freed

from the Commission's intensive surveillance regime. An extra year also confirmed for Portugal.

2 July 2013   Portugal plunged into crisis following the resignations of both its foreign and finance ministers and fears about the survival of the austerity-minded centre-right coalition. Yields on ten-year bonds rise to above 8% and domino effect felt across Europe.

7 July 2013   The IMF admits having made mistakes in handling the Greek debt crisis but argues that it would all have been better handled and cheaper if they had been allowed by the Europeans to restructure Greek debt upfront in 2010.

10 July 2013   The European Commission proposes a Single Resolution Mechanism to become operational in 2015. This would allow banks 'to be resolved quickly, efficiently, avoiding doubts in the impact on public finances and with rules that create certainty in the markets'. A Single Resolution Board under the guidance of the ECB would prepare the recommendation for the resolution of a bank and

oversee its implementation but decision to trigger a resolution would rest with the Commission.

18 July 2013   German Finance Minister Wolfgang Schäuble visits Greece and declares himself pleased with Greek efforts to handle the deficit and debt crisis.

26 July 2013   Eurozone officials agree to despatch next bail-out tranche of €4bn to Greece.

28 July 2013   Schäuble, in what is seen as a 'pre-election' address for the elections due in Germany in late September, insists that Greece will not be handed a second 'haircut'.

29 July 2013   Italian Prime Minister Enrico Letta expresses solidarity with Greece as he ends his two-day visit to the country and castigates the timing of the policy interventions imposed on Greece as well as their appropriateness.

29 July 2013   The EC third report on Greece's bail-out states that although improvement is still needed in many areas, the programme is 'broadly on track'. It forecasts a drop of 4.2% in GDP in 2013 followed by growth of 0.6% in 2014, 2.9% in 2015 and 3.7% in 2016.

31 July 2013	Greece receives a €4bn bail-out tranche. IMF warns that the country may need €11bn extra funds over next ten years and may require extra debt relief.
2 August 2013	Latest Irish data suggests that Irish deficit target for 2013 of 7.5% of GDP will be met. Target for 2014 set at 5.1%.
14 August 2013	Eurostat reports growth of 0.3% in the second quarter for the seventeen eurozone countries after six quarters of decline. Growth uneven, recovery in Germany and France contrasts with continued declines in the periphery countries.
18 August 2013	Greece dismisses chairperson of its privatisation agency HRADF for accepting a ride in the private aeroplane of the person who bought a major stake asset, the state lottery company, OPAP. He is the second chair to leave within six months. Targets for privatisation receipts for 2013 are reduced to €1.6bn from €2.6bn six months previously.
23 August 2013	IMF's working paper WP/13/182 assessing the impact and phasing of multi-year fiscal adjustment programmes admits that the

organisation was over-optimistic on potential growth forecasts for Greece.

25 August 2013 — The German and Greek finance ministers appear to agree that another €10bn of bail-out funds will be needed by Greece soon.

26 August 2013 — Greece announces its intention to return to the markets in a small way in 2014. Greece's current account balance is now close to zero compared with a deficit in 2008 of 15% of GDP.

26 August 2013 — Italian stocks fall and yields rise as coalition government remains under pressure.

2 September 2013 — Schäuble states in a debate in the German Bundestag that Greece's funding gap for a third bail-out is no more than €4–4.5bn.

22 September 2013 — The IMF, European Commission and ECB visit Greece to oversee progress of the 2015–16 budget. On 29 September, the troika halted the inspection temporarily 'to allow for the completion of technical work'.

22 September 2013 — Angela Merkel is re-elected German Chancellor but her coalition partner, the FDP, which believes in ultra-liberal economic policies, is defeated and returns no members to the Bundestag.

28 September 2013   Greek police arrest the leaders, a
                     number of MPs and officials of the
                     neo-Nazi Golden Dawn party on
                     charges of inciting violence.

INDEX

Also available from Biteback Publishing

PRISONOMICS
Vicky Pryce

In March 2013, Vicky Pryce was sentenced to eight
months in prison for accepting her ex-husband's
penalty points on her driving licence some ten years
earlier. After a very public trial, she was sent first to
the notorious Holloway and then to East Sutton Park,
an open prison in Kent. Inside, she kept a diary
documenting her views and experiences; from this
diary, *Prisonomics* was born.

Prisonomics is not only a personal account of
Pryce's experience in prison. It is also a compelling
analysis of both the economic and the very human
cost of keeping women behind bars.

336pp hardback, £16.99
Available from all good bookshops or order from
www.bitebackpublishing.com